Our Changing Environment, Grade K

T0383802

What if you could challenge your kindergartners to come up with a way to reduce human impact on the environment? With this volume in the *STEM Road Map Curriculum Series*, you can!

Our Changing Environment outlines a journey that will steer your students toward authentic problem solving while grounding them in integrated STEM disciplines. Like the other volumes in the series, this book is designed to meet the growing need to infuse real-world learning into K–12 classrooms.

This interdisciplinary, three-lesson module uses project- and problem-based learning to help students investigate the environment around them, with a focus on ways that humans can impact the environment. Working in teams, students will investigate various types of human impact on the environment (including pollution, littering, and habitat destruction), will participate in a classroom recycling program, and will explore the engineering design process as they devise ways to repurpose waste materials. To support this goal, students will do the following:

- Identify human impacts on the environment.

- Identify technological advances and tools that scientists use to learn about the changing environment, and use technology to gather data.

- Explain, discuss, and express concepts about the environment through development and design of a publication to report their scientific findings about the environment around the school.

- Chart and understand local weather patterns, and make connections between weather conditions and their observations of the environment.

- Identify and demonstrate recycling practices, including sorting materials and tracking amounts of materials recycled, and participate in a class recycling program.

The *STEM Road Map Curriculum Series* is anchored in the Next Generation Science Standards, the Common Core State Standards, and the Framework for 21st Century Learning. In-depth and flexible, *Our Changing Environment* can be used as a whole unit or in part to meet the needs of districts, schools, and teachers who are charting a course toward an integrated STEM approach.

Carla C. Johnson is Professor of Science Education in the College of Education and Office of Research and Innovation, and a Faculty Research Fellow at North Carolina State University in North Carolina, USA

Janet B. Walton is Senior Research Scholar at North Carolina State University in North Carolina, USA

Erin E. Peters-Burton is the Donna R. and David E. Sterling Endowed Professor in Science Education at George Mason University in Virginia, USA

THE STEM ROAD MAP CURRICULUM SERIES

Series editors: Carla C. Johnson, Janet B. Walton, and Erin E. Peters-Burton

Map out a journey that will steer your students toward authentic problem solving as you ground them in integrated STEM disciplines.

Co-published by Routledge and NSTA Press, in partnership with the National Science Teaching Association, this K–12 curriculum series is anchored in the Next Generation Science Standards, the Common Core State Standards, and the Framework for 21st Century Learning. It was developed to meet the growing need to infuse real-world STEM learning into classrooms.

Each book is an in-depth module that uses project- and problem-based learning. First, your students are presented with a challenge. Then, they apply what they learn using science, social studies, English language arts, and mathematics. Engaging and flexible, each volume can be used as a whole unit or in part to meet the needs of districts, schools, and teachers who are charting a course toward an integrated STEM approach.

Modules are available from NSTA Press and Routledge, and organized under the following themes. For an update listing of the volumes in the series, please visit https://www.routledge.com/STEM-Road-Map-Curriculum-Series/book-series/SRM (for titles co-published by Routledge and NSTA Press), or www.nsta.org/book-series/stem-road-map-curriculum (for titles published by NSTA Press).

Co-published by Routledge and NSTA Press:

Optimizing the Human Experience:

- Our Changing Environment, Grade K: STEM Road Map for Elementary School
- Genetically Modified Organisms, Grade 7: STEM Road Map for Middle School
- Rebuilding the Natural Environment, Grade 10: STEM Road Map for High School
- Mineral Resources, Grade 11: STEM Road Map for High School

Cause and Effect:

- Formation of the Earth, Grade 9: STEM Road Map for High School

Published by NSTA Press:

Innovation and Progress:

- Amusement Park of the Future, Grade 6: STEM Road Map for Elementary School
- Transportation in the Future, Grade 3: STEM Road Map for Elementary School
- Harnessing Solar Energy, Grade 4: STEM Road Map for Elementary School
- Wind Energy, Grade 5: STEM Road Map for Elementary School
- Construction Materials, Grade 11: STEM Road Map for High School

The Represented World:

- Patterns and the Plant World, Grade 1: STEM Road Map for Elementary School

- Investigating Environmental Changes, Grade 2: STEM Road Map for Elementary School
- Swing Set Makeover, Grade 3: STEM Road Map for Elementary School
- Rainwater Analysis, Grade 5: STEM Road Map for Elementary School
- Packaging Design, Grade 6: STEM Road Map for Middle School
- Improving Bridge Design, Grade 8: STEM Road Map for Middle School
- Radioactivity, Grade 11: STEM Road Map for High School
- Car Crashes, Grade 12: STEM Road Map for High School

Cause and Effect:

- Physics in Motion, Grade K: STEM Road Map for Elementary School
- Influence of Waves, Grade 1: STEM Road Map for Elementary School
- Natural Hazards, Grade 2: STEM Road Map for Elementary School
- Human Impacts on Our Climate, Grade 6: STEM Road Map for Middle School
- The Changing Earth, Grade 8: STEM Road Map for Middle School
- Healthy Living, Grade 10: STEM Road Map for High School

Our Changing Environment

Grade K

STEM Road Map
for Elementary School

Edited by Carla C. Johnson, Janet B. Walton, and
Erin E. Peters-Burton

Routledge
Taylor & Francis Group

NEW YORK AND LONDON

nsta Press
National Science Teaching Association

Cover images: icon © Shutterstock, map © Getty Images
Art and design for cover and interior adapted from NSTA Press.

First published 2022
by Routledge
605 Third Avenue, New York, NY 10158

and by Routledge
4 Park Square, Milton Park, Abingdon, Oxon, OX14 4RN

Routledge is an imprint of the Taylor & Francis Group, an informa business

A co-publication with NSTA Press.

Library of Congress Cataloging-in-Publication Data
Names: Johnson, Carla C., 1969– editor. | Walton, Janet B., 1968– editor. | Peters-Burton, Erin E., editor.
Title: Our changing environment. Grade K : STEM road map for elementary school /
    edited by Carla C. Johnson, Janet B. Walton, and Erin E. Peters-Burton.
Description: New York, NY : Routledge, 2022. | Series: STEM road map curriculum series |
    Includes bibliographical references and index.
Identifiers: LCCN 2021053114 | ISBN 9781032199801 (hardback) | ISBN 9781032199795 (paperback) |
    ISBN 9781003261728 (ebook)
Subjects: LCSH: Environmental sciences—Study and teaching (Kindergarten)—Activity programs. |
    Project method in teaching.
Classification: LCC GE77 .O87 2022 | DDC 372.35/7—dc23/eng/20220104
LC record available at https://lccn.loc.gov/2021053114

ISBN: 978-1-032-19980-1 (hbk)
ISBN: 978-1-032-19979-5 (pbk)
ISBN: 978-1-003-26172-8 (ebk)

DOI: 10.4324/9781003261728

Typeset in Palatino LT Std
by Apex CoVantage, LLC

Access the Support Material: www.routledge.com/9781032199795

CONTENTS

CONTENTS

ABOUT THE EDITORS AND AUTHORS

Dr. Carla C. Johnson is a Professor of Science Education and Office of Research and Innovation Faculty Research Fellow at NC State University. Dr. Johnson has served (2015–2021) as the director of research and evaluation for the Department of Defense–funded Army Educational Outreach Program (AEOP), a global portfolio of STEM education programs, competitions, and apprenticeships. She has been a leader in STEM education for the past decade, serving as the director of STEM Centers, editor of the School Science and Mathematics journal, and lead researcher for the evaluation of Tennessee's Race to the Top–funded STEM portfolio. Dr. Johnson has published over 200 articles, books, book chapters, and curriculum books focused on STEM education. She is a former science and social studies teacher and was the recipient of the 2013 Outstanding Science Teacher Educator of the Year award from the Association for Science Teacher Education (ASTE), the 2012 Award for Excellence in Integrating Science and Mathematics from the School Science and Mathematics Association (SSMA), the 2014 award for best paper on Implications of Research for Educational Practice from ASTE, and the 2006 Outstanding Early Career Scholar Award from SSMA. Her research focuses on STEM education policy implementation, effective science teaching, and integrated STEM approaches.

Dr. Janet B. Walton is a senior research scholar at NC State's College of Education in Raleigh, North Carolina. Formerly the STEM workforce program manager for Virginia's Region 2000 and founding director of the Future Focus Foundation, a nonprofit organization dedicated to enhancing the quality of STEM education in the region, she merges her economic development and education backgrounds to develop K–12 curricular materials that integrate real-life issues with sound cross-curricular content. Her research focus includes collaboration between schools and community stakeholders for STEM education, problem- and project- based learning pedagogies, online learning, and mixed methods research methodologies. She leverages this background to bring contextual STEM experiences into the classroom and provide students and educators with innovative resources and curricular materials. She is the former assistant director of evaluation of research and evaluation for the Department of Defense–funded Army Educational Outreach Program (AEOP), a global portfolio of STEM education programs, competitions, and apprenticeships and specializes in evaluation of STEM programs.

Dr. Erin E. Peters-Burton is the Donna R. and David E. Sterling endowed professor in science education at George Mason University in Fairfax, Virginia. She uses her experiences from 15 years as an engineer and secondary science, engineering, and mathematics teacher to develop research projects that directly inform classroom practice in science and engineering. Her research agenda is based on the idea that all students should build self-awareness of how they learn science and engineering. She works to help students see themselves as "science- minded" and help teachers create classrooms that support student skills to develop scientific knowledge. To accomplish this, she pursues research projects that investigate ways that students and teachers can use self-regulated learning theory in science and engineering, as well as how inclusive STEM schools can help students succeed. She received the Outstanding Science Teacher Educator of the Year award from ASTE in 2016 and a Teacher of Distinction Award and a Scholarly Achievement Award from George Mason University in 2012, and in 2010 she was named University Science Educator of the Year by the Virginia Association of Science Teachers.

Dr. Toni A. May is an associate professor of assessment, research, and statistics in the School of Education at Drexel University in Philadelphia. Dr. May's research concentrates on assessment and evaluation in education, with a focus on K–12 STEM.

Dr. Andrea R. Milner is the vice president and dean of academic affairs and an associate professor in the Teacher Education Department at Adrian College in Adrian, Michigan. A former early childhood and elementary teacher, Dr. Milner researches the effects constructivist classroom contextual factors have on student motivation and learning strategy use.

Dr. Tamara J. Moore is an associate professor of engineering education in the College of Engineering at Purdue University. Dr. Moore's research focuses on defining STEM integration through the use of engineering as the connection and investigating its power for student learning.

Dr. Vanessa B. Morrison is an associate professor in the Teacher Education Department at Adrian College. She is a former early childhood teacher and reading and language arts specialist whose research is focused on learning and teaching within a transdisciplinary framework.

ACKNOWLEDGMENTS

This module was developed as a part of the STEM Road Map project (Carla C. Johnson, principal investigator). The Purdue University College of Education, General Motors, and other sources provided funding for this project.

PART 1

THE STEM ROAD MAP

BACKGROUND, THEORY, AND PRACTICE

OVERVIEW OF THE *STEM ROAD MAP CURRICULUM SERIES*

Carla C. Johnson, Erin E. Peters-Burton, and Tamara J. Moore

The *STEM Road Map Curriculum Series* was conceptualized and developed by a team of STEM educators from across the United States in response to a growing need to infuse real-world learning contexts, delivered through authentic problem-solving pedagogy, into K–12 classrooms. The curriculum series is grounded in integrated STEM, which focuses on the integration of the STEM disciplines – science, technology, engineering, and mathematics – delivered across content areas, incorporating the Framework for 21st Century Learning along with grade-level-appropriate academic standards. The curriculum series begins in kindergarten, with a five-week instructional sequence that introduces students to the STEM themes and gives them grade-level-appropriate topics and real-world challenges or problems to solve. The series uses project-based and problem-based learning, presenting students with the problem or challenge during the first lesson, and then teaching them science, social studies, English language arts, mathematics, and other content, as they apply what they learn to the challenge or problem at hand.

Authentic assessment and differentiation are embedded throughout the modules. Each *STEM Road Map Curriculum Series* module has a lead discipline, which may be science, social studies, English language arts, or mathematics. All disciplines are integrated into each module, along with ties to engineering. Another key component is the use of STEM Research Notebooks to allow students to track their own learning progress. The modules are designed with a scaffolded approach, with increasingly complex concepts and skills introduced as students' progress through grade levels.

The developers of this work view the curriculum as a resource that is intended to be used either as a whole or in part to meet the needs of districts, schools, and teachers who are implementing an integrated STEM approach. A variety of implementation formats are possible, from using one stand- alone module at a given grade level to using all five modules to provide 25 weeks of instruction. Also, within each grade

DOI: 10.4324/9781003261728-2

band (K–2, 3–5, 6–8, 9–12), the modules can be sequenced in various ways to suit specific needs.

STANDARDS-BASED APPROACH

The *STEM Road Map Curriculum Series* is anchored in the *Next Generation Science Standards* (*NGSS*), the *Common Core State Standards for Mathematics* (*CCSS Mathematics*), the *Common Core State Standards for English Language Arts* (*CCSS ELA*), and the Framework for 21st Century Learning. Each module includes a detailed curriculum map that incorporates the associated standards from the particular area correlated to lesson plans. The STEM Road Map has very clear and strong connections to these academic standards, and each of the grade-level topics was derived from the mapping of the standards to ensure alignment among topics, challenges or problems, and the required academic standards for students. Therefore, the curriculum series takes a standards-based approach and is designed to provide authentic contexts for application of required knowledge and skills.

THEMES IN THE *STEM ROAD MAP CURRICULUM SERIES*

The K–12 STEM Road Map is organized around five real-world STEM themes that were generated through an examination of the big ideas and challenges for society included in STEM standards and those that are persistent dilemmas for current and future generations:

- Cause and Effect

- Innovation and Progress

- The Represented World

- Sustainable Systems

- Optimizing the Human Experience

These themes are designed as springboards for launching students into an exploration of real-world learning situated within big ideas. Most important, the five STEM Road Map themes serve as a framework for scaffolding STEM learning across the K–12 continuum.

The themes are distributed across the STEM disciplines so that they represent the big ideas in science (Cause and Effect; Sustainable Systems), technology (Innovation and Progress; Optimizing the Human Experience), engineering (Innovation and Progress; Sustainable Systems; Optimizing the Human Experience), and mathematics (The Represented World), as well as concepts and challenges in social studies and 21st century skills that are also excellent contexts for learning in English language arts. The process of developing themes began with the clustering of the *NGSS* performance expectations and the National Academy of Engineering's grand challenges for engineering, which led to the development of the challenge in each module and connections of the module activities to the *CCSS Mathematics* and *CCSS ELA* standards. We performed these mapping processes with large teams of experts and found that these five themes provided breadth, depth, and coherence to frame a high-quality STEM learning experience from kindergarten through 12th grade.

Cause and Effect

The concept of cause and effect is a powerful and pervasive notion in the STEM fields. It is the foundation of understanding how and why things happen as they do. Humans spend considerable effort and resources trying to understand the causes and effects of natural and designed phenomena to gain better control over events and the environment and to be prepared to react appropriately. Equipped with the knowledge of a specific cause-and-effect relationship, we can lead better lives or contribute to the community by altering the cause, leading to a different effect. For example, if a person recognizes that irresponsible energy consumption leads to global climate change, that person can act to remedy his or her contribution to the situation. Although cause and effect is a core idea in the STEM fields, it can actually be difficult to determine. Students should be capable of understanding not only when evidence points to cause and effect but also when evidence points to relationships but not direct causality. The major goal of education is to foster students to be empowered, analytic thinkers, capable of thinking through complex processes to make important decisions. Understanding causality, as well as when it cannot be determined, will help students become better consumers, global citizens, and community members.

Innovation and Progress

One of the most important factors in determining whether humans will have a positive future is innovation. Innovation is the driving force behind progress, which helps create possibilities that did not exist before. Innovation and progress are creative entities, but in the STEM fields, they are anchored by evidence and logic, and they use established concepts to move the STEM fields forward. In creating something new, students must consider what is already known in the STEM fields and apply this knowledge appropriately. When we innovate, we create value that was not there previously and create new conditions and possibilities for even more innovations. Students should consider how their innovations might affect progress and use their STEM thinking to change current human burdens to benefits. For example, if we develop more efficient cars that use by-products from another manufacturing industry, such as food processing, then we have used waste productively and reduced the need for the waste to be hauled away, an indirect benefit of the innovation.

The Represented World

When we communicate about the world we live in, how the world works, and how we can meet the needs of humans, sometimes we can use the actual phenomena to explain a concept. Sometimes, however, the concept is too big, too slow, too small, too fast, or too complex for us to explain using the actual phenomena, and we must use a representation or a model to help communicate the important features. We need representations and models such as graphs, tables, mathematical expressions, and diagrams because it makes our thinking visible. For example, when examining geologic time, we cannot actually observe the passage of such large chunks of time, so we create a timeline or a model that uses a proportional scale to visually illustrate how much time has passed for different eras. Another example may be something too complex for students at a particular grade level, such as explaining the p subshell orbitals of electrons to fifth graders. Instead, we use the Bohr model, which more closely represents the orbiting of planets and is accessible to fifth graders.

When we create models, they are helpful because they point out the most important features of a phenomenon. We also create representations of the world with mathematical functions, which help us change parameters to suit the situation. Creating representations of a phenomenon engages students because they are able to identify the important features of that phenomenon and communicate them directly. But because models are estimates of a phenomenon, they leave out some of the details, so it is important for students to evaluate their usefulness as well as their shortcomings.

Sustainable Systems

From an engineering perspective, the term *system* refers to the use of "concepts of component need, component interaction, systems interaction, and feedback. The interaction of subcomponents to produce a functional system is a common lens used by all engineering disciplines for understanding, analysis, and design." (Koehler, Bloom, and Binns 2013, p. 8). Systems can be either open (e.g., an ecosystem) or closed (e.g., a car battery). Ideally, a system should be sustainable, able to maintain equilibrium without much energy from outside the structure. Looking at a garden, we see flowers blooming, weeds sprouting, insects buzzing, and various forms of life living within its boundaries. This is an example of an ecosystem, a collection of living organisms that survive together, functioning as a system. The interaction of the organisms within the system and the influences of the environment (e.g., water, sunlight) can maintain the system for a period of time, thus demonstrating its ability to endure. Sustainability is a desirable feature of a system because it allows for existence of the entity in the long term.

In the STEM Road Map project, we identified different standards that we consider to be oriented toward systems that students should know and understand in the K–12 setting. These include ecosystems, the rock cycle, Earth processes (such as erosion, tectonics, ocean currents, weather phenomena), Earth-Sun-Moon cycles, heat transfer, and the interaction among the geosphere, biosphere, hydrosphere, and atmosphere. Students and teachers should understand that we live in a world of systems that are not independent of each other, but rather are intrinsically linked such that a disruption in one part of a system will have reverberating effects on other parts of the system.

Optimizing the Human Experience

Science, technology, engineering, and mathematics as disciplines have the capacity to continuously improve the ways humans live, interact, and find meaning in the world, thus working to optimize the human experience. This idea has two components: being more suited to our environment and being more fully human. For example, the progression of STEM ideas can help humans create solutions to complex problems, such as improving ways to access water sources, designing energy sources with minimal impact on our environment, developing new ways of communication and expression, and building efficient shelters. STEM ideas can also provide access to the secrets and wonders of nature. Learning in STEM requires students to think logically and systematically, which is a way of knowing the world that is markedly different from knowing the world as an artist. When students can employ various ways of knowing and understand when it is appropriate to use a different way of knowing or integrate ways of knowing, they are fully experiencing the best of what it is to be human. The problem-based learning scenarios provided in the STEM Road Map help students develop ways of thinking like STEM professionals as they ask questions and design solutions. They learn to optimize the human experience by innovating improvements in the designed world in which they live.

THE NEED FOR AN INTEGRATED STEM APPROACH

At a basic level, STEM stands for science, technology, engineering, and mathematics. Over the past decade, however, STEM has evolved to have a much broader scope and implications. Now, educators and policy makers refer to STEM as not only a concentrated area for investing in the future of the United States and other nations but also as a domain and mechanism for educational reform. The good intentions of the recent decade-plus of focus on accountability and increased testing has resulted in significant decreases not only in instructional time for teaching science and social studies but also in the flexibility of teachers to promote authentic, problem solving–focused classroom environments. The shift has had a detrimental impact on student acquisition of vitally important skills, which many refer to as 21st century skills, and often the ability of students to "think." Further, schooling has become increasingly siloed into compartments of mathematics, science, English language, arts and social studies, lacking any of the

connections that are overwhelmingly present in the real world around children. Students have experienced school as content provided in boxes that must be memorized, devoid of any real-world context, and often have little understanding of why they are learning these things.

STEM-focused projects, curriculum, activities, and schools have emerged as a means to address these challenges. However, most of these efforts have continued to focus on the individual STEM disciplines (predominantly science and engineering) through more STEM classes and after-school programs in a "STEM enhanced" approach (Breiner et al. 2012). But in traditional and STEM enhanced approaches, there is little to no focus on other disciplines that are integral to the context of STEM in the real world. Integrated STEM education, on the other hand, infuses the learning of important STEM content and concepts with a much-needed emphasis on 21st century skills and a problem- and project-based pedagogy that more closely mirrors the real-world setting for society's challenges. It incorporates social studies, English language arts, and the arts as pivotal and necessary (Johnson 2013; Rennie, Venville, and Wallace 2012; Roehrig et al. 2012).

Framework for Stem Integration in The Classroom

The *STEM Road Map Curriculum Series* is grounded in the Framework for STEM Integration in the Classroom as conceptualized by Moore, Guzey, and Brown (2014) and Moore et al. (2014). The framework has six elements, described in the context of how they are used in the *STEM Road Map Curriculum Series* as follows:

1. The STEM Road Map contexts are meaningful to students and provide motivation to engage with the content. Together, these allow students to have different ways to enter into the challenge.

2. The STEM Road Map modules include engineering design that allows students to design technologies (i.e., products that are part of the designed world) for a compelling purpose.

3. The STEM Road Map modules provide students with the opportunities to learn from failure and redesign based on the lessons learned.

4. The STEM Road Map modules include standards-based disciplinary content as the learning objectives.

5. The STEM Road Map modules include student-centered pedagogies that allow students to grapple with the content, tie their ideas to the context, and learn to think for themselves as they deepen their conceptual knowledge.

6. The STEM Road Map modules emphasize 21st century skills and, in particular, highlight communication and teamwork.

All of the STEM Road Map modules incorporate these six elements; however, the level of emphasis on each of these elements varies based on the challenge or problem in each module.

THE NEED FOR THE *STEM ROAD MAP CURRICULUM SERIES*

As focus is increasing on integrated STEM, and additional schools and programs decide to move their curriculum and instruction in this direction, there is a need for high- quality, research-based curriculum designed with integrated STEM at the core. Several good resources are available to help teachers infuse engineering or more STEM enhanced approaches, but no curriculum exists that spans K–12 with an integrated STEM focus. The next chapter provides detailed information about the specific pedagogy, instructional strategies, and learning theory on which the *STEM Road Map Curriculum Series* is grounded.

REFERENCES

Breiner, J., M. Harkness, C. C. Johnson, and C. Koehler. 2012. What is STEM? A discussion about conceptions of STEM in education and partnerships. *School Science and Mathematics* 112 (1): 3–11.

Johnson, C. C. 2013. Conceptualizing integrated STEM education: Editorial. *School Science and Mathematics* 113 (8): 367–368.

Koehler, C. M., M. A. Bloom, and I. C. Binns. 2013. Lights, camera, action: Developing a methodology to document mainstream films' portrayal of nature of science and scientific inquiry. *Electronic Journal of Science Education* 17 (2).

Moore, T. J., S. S. Guzey, and A. Brown. 2014. Greenhouse design to increase habitable land: An engineering unit. *Science Scope* 51–57.

Moore, T. J., M. S. Stohlmann, H.-H. Wang, K. M. Tank, A. W. Glancy, and G. H. Roehrig. 2014. Implementation and integration of engineering in K–12 STEM education. In *Engineering in pre- college settings: Synthesizing research, policy, and practices,* ed. S. Purzer, J. Strobel, and M. Cardella, 35–60. West Lafayette, IN: Purdue Press.

Rennie, L., G. Venville, and J. Wallace. 2012. *Integrating science, technology, engineering, and mathematics: Issues, reflections, and ways forward.* New York: Routledge.

Roehrig, G. H., T. J. Moore, H. H. Wang, and M. S. Park. 2012. Is adding the E enough? Investigating the impact of K–12 engineering standards on the implementation of STEM integration. *School Science and Mathematics* 112 (1): 31–44.

STRATEGIES USED IN THE *STEM ROAD MAP CURRICULUM SERIES*

Erin E. Peters-Burton, Carla C. Johnson, Toni A. May, and Tamara J. Moore

The *STEM Road Map Curriculum Series* uses what has been identified through research as best-practice pedagogy, including embedded formative assessment strategies throughout each module. This chapter briefly describes the key strategies that are employed in the series.

PROJECT- AND PROBLEM-BASED LEARNING

Each module in the *STEM Road Map Curriculum Series* uses either project-based learning or problem-based learning to drive the instruction. Project-based learning begins with a driving question to guide student teams in addressing a contextualized local or community problem or issue. The outcome of project-based instruction is a product that is conceptualized, designed, and tested through a series of scaffolded learning experiences (Blumenfeld et al. 1991; Krajcik and Blumenfeld 2006). Problem-based learning is often grounded in a fictitious scenario, challenge, or problem (Barell 2006; Lambros 2004). On the first day of instruction within the unit, student teams are provided with the context of the problem. Teams work through a series of activities and use open-ended research to develop their potential solution to the problem or challenge, which need not be a tangible product (Johnson 2003).

ENGINEERING DESIGN PROCESS

The *STEM Road Map Curriculum Series* uses engineering design as a way to facilitate integrated STEM within the modules. The engineering design process (EDP) is depicted in Figure 2.1 (p. 10). It highlights two major aspects of engineering design – problem scoping and solution generation – and six specific components of

DOI: 10.4324/9781003261728-3

Figure 2.1. Engineering Design Process

Engineering Design Process
A way to improve

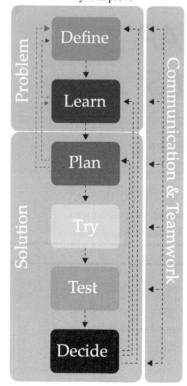

working toward a design: define the problem, learn about the problem, plan a solution, try the solution, test the solution, decide whether the solution is good enough. It also shows that communication and teamwork are involved throughout the entire process. As the arrows in the figure indicate, the order in which the components of engineering design are addressed depends on what becomes needed as designers progress through the EDP. Designers must communicate and work in teams throughout the process. The EDP is iterative, meaning that components of the process can be repeated as needed until the design is good enough to present to the client as a potential solution to the problem.

Problem scoping is the process of gathering and analyzing information to deeply understand the engineering design problem. It includes defining the problem and learning about the problem. Defining the problem includes identifying the problem, the client, and the end user of the design. The client is the person (or people) who hired the designers to do the work, and the end user is the person (or people) who will use the final design. The designers must also identify the criteria and the constraints of the problem. The criteria are the things the client wants from the solution, and the constraints are the things that limit the possible solutions. The designers must spend significant time learning about the problem, which can include activities such as the following:

- Reading informational texts and researching about relevant concepts or contexts

- Identifying and learning about needed mathematical and scientific skills, knowledge, and tools

- Learning about things done previously to solve similar problems

- Experimenting with possible materials that could be used in the design

Problem scoping also allows designers to consider how to measure the success of the design in addressing specific criteria and staying within the constraints over multiple iterations of solution generation.

Solution generation includes planning a solution, trying the solution, testing the solution, and deciding whether the solution is good enough. Planning the solution includes generating many design ideas that both address the criteria and meet the constraints. Here the designers must consider what was learned about the problem during problem scoping. Design plans include clear communication of design ideas through media such as notebooks, blueprints, schematics, or storyboards. They also include details about the design, such as measurements, materials, colors, costs of materials, instructions for how things fit together, and sets of directions. Making the decision about which design idea to move forward involves considering the trade-offs of each design idea.

Once a clear design plan is in place, the designers must try the solution. Trying the solution includes developing a prototype (a testable model) based on the plan generated. The prototype might be something physical or a process to accomplish a goal. This component of design requires that the designers consider the risk involved in implementing the design. The prototype developed must be tested. Testing the solution includes conducting fair tests that verify whether the plan is a solution that is good enough to meet the client and end user needs and wants. Data need to be collected about the results of the tests of the prototype, and these data should be used to make evidence-based decisions regarding the design choices made in the plan. Here, the designers must again consider the criteria and constraints for the problem.

Using the data gathered from the testing, the designers must decide whether the solution is good enough to meet the client and end user needs and wants by assessment based on the criteria and constraints. Here, the designers must justify or reject design decisions based on the background research gathered while learning about the problem and on the evidence gathered during the testing of the solution. The designers must now decide whether to present the current solution to the client as a possibility or to do more iterations of design on the solution. If they decide that improvements need to be made to the solution, the designers must decide if there is more that needs to be understood about the problem, client, or end user; if another design idea should be tried; or if more planning needs to be conducted on the same design. One way or another, more work needs to be done.

Throughout the process of designing a solution to meet a client's needs and wants, designers work in teams and must communicate to each other, the client, and likely the end user. Teamwork is important in engineering design because multiple perspectives and differing skills and knowledge are valuable when working to solve problems. Communication is key to the success of the designed solution. Designers must communicate their ideas clearly using many different representations, such as text in an engineering notebook, diagrams, flowcharts, technical briefs, or memos to the client.

LEARNING CYCLE

The same format for the learning cycle is used in all grade levels throughout the STEM Road Map, so that students engage in a variety of activities to learn about phenomena in the modules thoroughly and have consistent experiences in the problem- and

project- based learning modules. Expectations for learning by younger students are not as high as for older students, but the format of the progression of learning is the same. Students who have learned with curriculum from the STEM Road Map in early grades know what to expect in later grades. The learning cycle consists of five parts – Introductory Activity/Engagement, Activity/Exploration, Explanation, Elaboration/Application of Knowledge, and Evaluation/Assessment – and is based on the empirically tested 5E model from BSCS (Bybee et al. 2006).

In the Introductory Activity/Engagement phase, teachers introduce the module challenge and use a unique approach designed to pique students' curiosity. This phase gets students to start thinking about what they already know about the topic and begin wondering about key ideas. The Introductory Activity/Engagement phase positions students to be confident about what they are about to learn, because they have prior knowledge, and clues them into what they don't yet know.

In the Activity/Exploration phase, the teacher sets up activities in which students experience a deeper look at the topics that were introduced earlier. Students engage in the activities and generate new questions or consider possibilities using preliminary investigations. Students work independently, in small groups, and in whole-group settings to conduct investigations, resulting in common experiences about the topic and skills involved in the real-world activities. Teachers can assess students' development of concepts and skills based on the common experiences during this phase.

During the Explanation phase, teachers direct students' attention to concepts they need to understand and skills they need to possess to accomplish the challenge. Students participate in activities to demonstrate their knowledge and skills to this point, and teachers can pinpoint gaps in student knowledge during this phase.

In the Elaboration/Application of Knowledge phase, teachers present students with activities that engage in higher-order thinking to create depth and breadth of student knowledge, while connecting ideas across topics within and across STEM. Students apply what they have learned thus far in the module to a new context or elaborate on what they have learned about the topic to a deeper level of detail.

In the last phase, Evaluation/Assessment, teachers give students summative feedback on their knowledge and skills as demonstrated through the challenge. This is not the only point of assessment (as discussed in the section on Embedded Formative Assessments), but it is an assessment of the culmination of the knowledge and skills for the module. Students demonstrate their cognitive growth at this point and reflect on how far they have come since the beginning of the module. The challenges are designed to be multidimensional in the ways students must collaborate and communicate their new knowledge.

STEM RESEARCH NOTEBOOK

One of the main components of the *STEM Road Map Curriculum Series* is the STEM Research Notebook, a place for students to capture their ideas, questions, observations, reflections, evidence of progress, and other items associated with their daily work. At the beginning of each module, the teacher walks students through the setup of the STEM Research Notebook, which could be a three-ring binder, composition book, or spiral notebook. You may wish to have students create divided sections so that they can easily access work from various disciplines during the module. Electronic notebooks kept on student devices are also acceptable and encouraged. Students will develop their own table of contents and create chapters in the notebook for each module.

Each lesson in the *STEM Road Map Curriculum Series* includes one or more prompts that are designed for inclusion in the STEM Research Notebook and appear as questions or statements that the teacher assigns to students. These prompts require students to apply what they have learned across the lesson to solve the big problem or challenge for that module. Each lesson is designed to meaningfully refer students to the larger problem or challenge they have been assigned to solve with their teams. The STEM Research Notebook is designed to be a key formative assessment tool, as students' daily entries provide evidence of what they are learning. The notebook can be used as a mechanism for dialogue between the teacher and students, as well as for peer and self-evaluation.

The use of the STEM Research Notebook is designed to scaffold student notebooking skills across the grade bands in the *STEM Road Map Curriculum Series*. In the early grades, children learn how to organize their daily work in the notebook as a way to collect their products for future reference. In elementary school, students structure their notebooks to integrate background research along with their daily work and lesson prompts. In the upper grades (middle and high school), students expand their use of research and data gathering through team discussions to more closely mirror the work of STEM experts in the real world.

THE ROLE OF ASSESSMENT IN THE *STEM ROAD MAP CURRICULUM SERIES*

Starting in the middle years and continuing into secondary education, the word *assessment* typically brings grades to mind. These grades may take the form of a letter or a percentage, but they typically are used as a representation of a student's content mastery. If well thought out and implemented, however, classroom assessment can offer teachers, parents, and students valuable information about student learning and misconceptions that does not necessarily come in the form of a grade (Popham 2013).

The *STEM Road Map Curriculum Series* provides a set of assessments for each module. Teachers are encouraged to use assessment information for more than just assigning grades to students. Instead, assessments of activities requiring students to actively engage in their learning, such as student journaling in STEM Research Notebooks, collaborative presentations, and constructing graphic organizers, should be used to move student learning forward. Whereas other curriculum with assessments may include

objective-type (multiple-choice or matching) tests, quizzes, or worksheets, we have intentionally avoided these forms of assessments to better align assessment strategies with teacher instruction and student learning techniques. Since the focus of this book is on project- or problem-based STEM curriculum and instruction that focuses on higher-level thinking skills, appropriate and authentic performance assessments were developed to elicit the most reliable and valid indication of growth in student abilities (Brookhart and Nitko 2008).

Comprehensive Assessment System

Assessment throughout all STEM Road Map curriculum modules acts as a comprehensive system in which formative and summative assessments work together to provide teachers with high-quality information on student learning. Formative assessment occurs when the teacher finds out formally or informally what a student knows about a smaller, defined concept or skill and provides timely feedback to the student about his or her level of proficiency. Summative assessments occur when students have performed all activities in the module and are given a cumulative performance evaluation in which they demonstrate their growth in learning.

A comprehensive assessment system can be thought of as akin to a sporting event. Formative assessments are the practices: it is important to accomplish them consistently, they provide feedback to help students improve their learning, and making mistakes can be worthwhile if students are given an opportunity to learn from them. Summative assessments are the competitions: students need to be prepared to perform at the best of their ability. Without multiple opportunities to practice skills along the way through formative assessments, students will not have the best chance of demonstrating growth in abilities through summative assessments (Black and Wiliam 1998).

Embedded Formative Assessments

Formative assessments in this module serve two main purposes: to provide feedback to students about their learning and to provide important information for the teacher to inform immediate instructional needs. Providing feedback to students is particularly important when conducting problem- or project-based learning because students take on much of the responsibility for learning, and teachers must facilitate student learning in an informed way. For example, if students are required to conduct research for the Activity/Exploration phase but are not familiar with what constitutes a reliable resource, they may develop misconceptions based on poor information. When a teacher monitors this learning through formative assessments and provides specific feedback related to the instructional goals, students are less likely to develop incomplete or incorrect conceptions in their independent investigations. By using formative assessment to detect problems in student learning and then acting on this information, teachers help move student learning forward through these teachable moments.

Formative assessments come in a variety of formats. They can be informal, such as asking students probing questions related to student knowledge or tasks or simply observing students engaged in an activity to gather information about student skills. Formative assessments can also be formal, such as a written quiz or a laboratory practical.

Regardless of the type, three key steps must be completed when using formative assessments (Sondergeld, Bell, and Leusner 2010). First, the assessment is delivered to students so that teachers can collect data. Next, teachers analyze the data (student responses) to determine student strengths and areas that need additional support. Finally, teachers use the results from information collected to modify lessons and create learning environments that reinforce weak points in student learning. If student learning information is not used to modify instruction, the assessment cannot be considered formative in nature. Formative assessments can be about content, science process skills, or even learning skills. When a formative assessment focuses on content, it assesses student knowledge about the disciplinary core ideas from the *Next Generation Science Standards* (*NGSS*) or content objectives from *Common Core State Standards for Mathematics* (*CCSS Mathematics*) or *Common Core State Standards for English Language Arts* (*CCSS ELA*). Content-focused formative assessments ask students questions about declarative knowledge regarding the concepts they have been learning. Process skills formative assessments examine the extent to which a student can perform science and engineering practices from the *NGSS* or process objectives from *CCSS Mathematics* or *CCSS ELA*, such as constructing an argument. Learning skills can also be assessed formatively by asking students to reflect on the ways they learn best during a module and identify ways they could have learned more.

Assessment Maps

Assessment maps or blueprints can be used to ensure alignment between classroom instruction and assessment. If what students are learning in the classroom is not the same as the content on which they are assessed, the resultant judgment made on student learning will be invalid (Brookhart and Nitko 2008). Therefore, the issue of instruction and assessment alignment is critical. The assessment map for this book (found in Chapter 3) indicates by lesson whether the assessment should be completed as a group or on an individual basis, identifies the assessment as formative or summative in nature, and aligns the assessment with its corresponding learning objectives.

Note that the module includes far more formative assessments than summative assessments. This is done intentionally to provide students with multiple opportunities to practice their learning of new skills before completing a summative assessment. Note also that formative assessments are used to collect information on only one or two learning objectives at a time so that potential relearning or instructional modifications can focus on smaller and more manageable chunks of information. Conversely,

summative assessments in the module cover many more learning objectives, as they are traditionally used as final markers of student learning. This is not to say that information collected from summative assessments cannot or should not be used formatively. If teachers find that gaps in student learning persist after a summative assessment is completed, it is important to revisit these existing misconceptions or areas of weakness before moving on (Black et al. 2003).

SELF-REGULATED LEARNING THEORY IN THE STEM ROAD MAP MODULES

Many learning theories are compatible with the STEM Road Map modules, such as constructivism, situated cognition, and meaningful learning. However, we feel that the self-regulated learning theory (SRL) aligns most appropriately (Zimmerman 2000). SRL requires students to understand that thinking needs to be motivated and managed (Ritchhart, Church, and Morrison 2011). The STEM Road Map modules are student centered and are designed to provide students with choices, concrete hands-on experiences, and opportunities to see and make connections, especially across subjects (Eliason and Jenkins 2012; NAEYC 2016). Additionally, SRL is compatible with the modules because it fosters a learning environment that supports students' motivation, enables students to become aware of their own learning strategies, and requires reflection on learning while experiencing the module (Peters and Kitsantas 2010).

The theory behind SRL (see Figure 2.2) explains the different processes that students engage in before, during, and after a learning task. Because SRL is a cyclical learning process, the accomplishment of one cycle develops strategies for the next learning cycle. This cyclic way of learning aligns with the various sections in the STEM Road Map lesson plans on Introductory Activity/ Engagement, Activity/ Exploration, Explanation, Elaboration/Application of Knowledge, and Evaluation/Assessment. Since the students engaged in a module take on much of the responsibility for learning, this theory also provides guidance for teachers to keep students on the right track.

Figure 2.2. SRL Theory

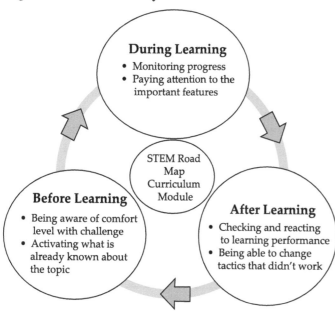

Source: Adapted from Zimmerman 2000.

The remainder of this section explains how SRL theory is embedded within the five sections of each module and points out ways to support students in becoming independent learners of STEM while productively functioning in collaborative teams. For an overview of how SRL processes incorporated specifically into the Our Changing Environment module, see Table 3.2 on p. 30.

Before Learning: Setting the Stage

Before attempting a learning task such as the STEM Road Map modules, teachers should develop an understanding of their students' level of comfort with the process of accomplishing the learning and determine what they already know about the topic. When students are comfortable with attempting a learning task, they tend to take more risks in learning and as a result achieve deeper learning (Bandura 1986).

The STEM Road Map curriculum modules are designed to foster excitement from the very beginning. Each module has an Introductory Activity/Engagement section that introduces the overall topic from a unique and exciting perspective, engaging the students to learn more so that they can accomplish the challenge. The Introductory Activity also has a design component that helps teachers assess what students already know about the topic of the module. In addition to the deliberate designs in the lesson plans to support SRL, teachers can support a high level of student comfort with the learning challenge by finding out if students have ever accomplished the same kind of task and, if so, asking them to share what worked well for them.

During Learning: Staying the Course

Some students fear inquiry learning because they aren't sure what to do to be successful (Peters 2010). However, the STEM Road Map curriculum modules are embedded with tools to help students pay attention to knowledge and skills that are important for the learning task and to check student understanding along the way. One of the most important processes for learning is the ability for learners to monitor their own progress while performing a learning task (Peters 2012). The modules allow students to monitor their progress with tools such as the STEM Research Notebooks, in which they record what they know and can check whether they have acquired a complete set of knowledge and skills. The STEM Road Map modules support inquiry strategies that include previewing, questioning, predicting, clarifying, observing, discussing, and journaling (Morrison and Milner 2014). Through the use of technology throughout the modules, inquiry is supported by providing students access to resources and data while enabling them to process information, report the findings, collaborate, and develop 21st century skills.

It is important for teachers to encourage students to have an open mind about alter- native solutions and procedures (Milner and Sondergeld 2015) when working through the STEM Road Map curriculum modules. Novice learners can have difficulty

knowing what to pay attention to and tend to treat each possible avenue for information as equal (Benner 1984). Teachers are the mentors in a classroom and can point out ways for students to approach learning during the Activity/Exploration, Explanation, and Elaboration/Application of Knowledge portions of the lesson plans to ensure that students pay attention to the important concepts and skills throughout the module. For example, if a student is to demonstrate conceptual awareness of motion when working on roller coaster research, but the student has misconceptions about motion, the teacher can step in and redirect student learning.

After Learning: Knowing What Works

The classroom is a busy place, and it may often seem that there is no time for self-reflection on learning. Although skipping this reflective process may save time in the short term, it reduces the ability to take into account things that worked well and things that didn't so that teaching the module may be improved next time. In the long run, SRL skills are critical for students to become independent learners who can adapt to new situations. By investing the time it takes to teach students SRL skills, teachers can save time later, because students will be able to apply methods and approaches for learning that they have found effective to new situations. In the Evaluation/Assessment portion of the STEM Road Map curriculum modules, as well as in the formative assessments throughout the modules, two processes in the after-learning phase are supported: evaluating one's own performance and accounting for ways to adapt tactics that didn't work well. Students have many opportunities to self-assess in formative assessments, both in groups and individually, using the rubrics provided in the modules.

The designs of the *NGSS* and *CCSS* allow for students to learn in diverse ways, and the STEM Road Map curriculum modules emphasize that students can use a variety of tactics to complete the learning process. For example, students can use STEM Research Notebooks to record what they have learned during the various research activities. Notebook entries might include putting objectives in students' own words, compiling their prior learning on the topic, documenting new learning, providing proof of what they learned, and reflecting on what they felt successful doing and what they felt they still needed to work on. Perhaps students didn't realize that they were supposed to connect what they already knew with what they learned. They could record this and would be prepared in the next learning task to begin connecting prior learning with new learning.

SAFETY IN STEM

Student safety is a primary consideration in all subjects but is an area of particular concern in science, where students may interact with unfamiliar tools and materials that may pose additional safety risks. It is important to implement safety practices within the context of STEM investigations, whether in a classroom laboratory or in the field.

When you keep safety in mind as a teacher, you avoid many potential issues with the lesson while also protecting your students.

STEM safety practices encompass things considered in the typical science classroom. Ensure that students are familiar with basic safety considerations, such as wearing protective equipment (e.g., safety glasses or goggles and latex-free gloves) and taking care with sharp objects, and know emergency exit procedures. Teachers should learn beforehand the locations of the safety eyewash, fume hood, fire extinguishers, and emergency shut-off switch in the classroom and how to use them. Also be aware of any school or district safety policies that are in place and apply those that align with the work being conducted in the lesson. It is important to review all safety procedures annually.

STEM investigations should always be supervised. Each lesson in the modules includes teacher guidelines for applicable safety procedures that should be followed. Before each investigation, teachers should go over these safety procedures with the student teams. Some STEM focus areas such as engineering require that students can demonstrate how to properly use equipment in the maker space before the teacher allows them to proceed with the lesson.

Information about classroom science safety, including a safety checklist for science classrooms, general lab safety recommendations, and links to other science safety resources, is available at the Council of State Science Supervisors (CSSS) website at *www.csss-science. org/safety.shtml.* The National Science Teaching Association (NSTA) provides a list of science rules and regulations, including standard operating procedures for lab safety, and a safety acknowledgment form for students and parents or guardians to sign. You can access these resources at http://static.nsta.org/pdfs/ SafetyInTheScienceClassroom.pdf. In addition, NSTA's Safety in the Science Classroom web page (*www.nsta.org/safety*) has numerous links to safety resources, including papers written by the NSTA Safety Advisory Board.

Disclaimer: The safety precautions for each activity are based on use of the recommended materials and instructions, legal safety standards, and better professional practices. Using alternative materials or procedures for these activities may jeopardize the level of safety and therefore is at the user's own risk.

REFERENCES

Bandura, A. 1986. *Social foundations of thought and action: A social cognitive theory.* Englewood Cliffs, NJ: Prentice-Hall.

Barell, J. 2006. *Problem-based learning: An inquiry approach.* Thousand Oaks, CA: Corwin Press.

Benner, P. 1984. *From novice to expert: Excellence and power in clinical nursing practice.* Menlo Park, CA: Addison-Wesley Publishing Company.

Black, P., C. Harrison, C. Lee, B. Marshall, and D. Wiliam. 2003. *Assessment for learning: Putting it into practice.* Berkshire, UK: Open University Press.

Black, P., and D. Wiliam. 1998. Inside the black box: Raising standards through classroom assessment. *Phi Delta Kappan* 80 (2): 139–148.

Blumenfeld, P., E. Soloway, R. Marx, J. Krajcik, M. Guzdial, and A. Palincsar. 1991. Motivating project-based learning: Sustaining the doing, supporting learning. *Educational Psychologist* 26 (3): 369–398.

Brookhart, S. M., and A. J. Nitko. 2008. *Assessment and grading in classrooms.* Upper Saddle River, NJ: Pearson.

Bybee, R., J. Taylor, A. Gardner, P. Van Scotter, J. Carlson, A. Westbrook, and N. Landes. 2006. *The BSCS 5E instructional model: Origins and effectiveness.* http://science.education.nih.gov/houseofreps.nsf/b82d55fa138783c2852572c9004f5566/$FILE/Appendix?D.pdf.

Eliason, C. F., and L. T. Jenkins. 2012. *A practical guide to early childhood curriculum.* 9th ed. New York: Merrill.

Johnson, C. 2003. Bioterrorism is real-world science: Inquiry-based simulation mirrors real life. *Science Scope* 27 (3): 19–23.

Krajcik, J., and P. Blumenfeld. 2006. Project-based learning. In *The Cambridge handbook of the learning sciences,* ed. R. Keith Sawyer, 317–334. New York: Cambridge University Press.

Lambros, A. 2004. *Problem-based learning in middle and high school classrooms: A teacher's guide to implementation.* Thousand Oaks, CA: Corwin Press.

Milner, A. R., and T. Sondergeld. 2015. Gifted urban middle school students: The inquiry continuum and the nature of science. *National Journal of Urban Education and Practice* 8 (3): 442–461.

Morrison, V., and A. R. Milner. 2014. Literacy in support of science: A closer look at cross-curricular instructional practice. *Michigan Reading Journal* 46 (2): 42–56.

National Association for the Education of Young Children (NAEYC). 2016. Developmentally appropriate practice position statements. www.naeyc.org/positionstatements/dap.

Peters, E. E. 2010. Shifting to a student-centered science classroom: An exploration of teacher and student changes in perceptions and practices. *Journal of Science Teacher Education* 21 (3): 329–349.

Peters, E. E. 2012. Developing content knowledge in students through explicit teaching of the nature of science: Influences of goal setting and self-monitoring. *Science and Education* 21 (6): 881–898.

Peters, E. E., and A. Kitsantas. 2010. The effect of nature of science metacognitive prompts on science students' content and nature of science knowledge, metacognition, and self-regulatory efficacy. *School Science and Mathematics* 110: 382–396.

Popham, W. J. 2013. *Classroom assessment: What teachers need to know.* 7th ed. Upper Saddle River, NJ: Pearson.

Ritchhart, R., M. Church, and K. Morrison. 2011. *Making thinking visible: How to promote engagement, understanding, and independence for all learners.* San Francisco, CA: Jossey-Bass.

Sondergeld, T. A., C. A. Bell, and D. M. Leusner. 2010. Understanding how teachers engage in formative assessment. *Teaching and Learning* 24 (2): 72–86.

Zimmerman, B. J. 2000. Attaining self-regulation: A social-cognitive perspective. In *Handbook of self-regulation*, ed. M. Boekaerts, P. Pintrich, and M. Zeidner, 13–39. San Diego: Academic Press.

PART 2

OUR CHANGING ENVIRONMENT

STEM ROAD MAP MODULE

OUR CHANGING ENVIRONMENT MODULE OVERVIEW

Vanessa B. Morrison, Andrea R. Milner, Janet B. Walton,
Carla C. Johnson and Erin E. Peters-Burton

THEME: Optimizing the Human Condition

LEAD DISCIPLINES: English Language Arts and Science

MODULE SUMMARY

In this module, students will investigate the environment around them with a focus on ways that humans can impact the environment. Students will investigate various types of pollution, will participate in a classroom recycling program, and will explore the engineering design process as they devise ways to repurpose waste materials. Through walking tours and observations of the school neighborhood and local weather, students will collect data about the environment on a local level and will create a plan for how the class can help care for the environment. Students will synthesize their learning during the module to publish a newspaper or blog targeted toward other kindergartners, highlighting the environmental data they have identified and proposing ways that people can protect the environment (adapted from Koehler, Bloom, and Milner, 2015; see https://www.routledge.com/products/9781138804234).

ESTABLISHED GOALS AND OBJECTIVES

At the conclusion of this module, students will be able to do the following:

- Identify the basic needs of living things
- Identify features of habitats
- Identify human impacts on environment.
- Understand that there are various causes for environmental changes

DOI: 10.4324/9781003261728-5

- Understand that there are various solutions for environmental changes

- Design and produce a publication (class blog or newsletter) to report their findings

- Explain/discuss/express concepts about the environment through the development of a school newspaper or blog to be distributed to other kindergarten classes

- Understand local weather patterns and be able to make connections between the weather and local environmental conditions

- Identify and demonstrate recycling practices, including sorting materials and tracking amounts of materials recycled

- Identify several ways that people can impact the natural environment

- Identify recycling as one way to reduce humans' impact on the environment and participate in a class recycling program

CHALLENGE OR PROBLEM FOR STUDENTS TO SOLVE: THE ENVIRONMENTAL EXPLORERS CHALLENGE

In this module, students are challenged to act as environmental explorers. Student teams will create a school newspaper or blog for other kindergarten students about the environment in the school neighborhood (Koehler et al., 2015). Students will focus on human impacts on the environment such as littering, pollution, habitat destruction, or other activities that cause visible environmental changes in the short term and will include information in their publication about how people can care for the environment. *Driving Question:* How can we care for the environment?

CONTENT STANDARDS ADDRESSED IN THIS STEM ROAD MAP MODULE

A full listing with descriptions of the standards this module addresses can be found in Appendix C. Listings of the particular standards addressed within lessons are provided in a table for each lesson in Chapter 4.

STEM RESEARCH NOTEBOOK

Each student should maintain a STEM Research Notebook, which will serve as a place for students to organize their work throughout this module (see pp. 12–13 for more general discussion on setup and use of this notebook). All written work in the module should be included in the notebook, including records of students' thoughts and ideas, fictional accounts based on the concepts in the module, and records of student progress through the EDP. The notebooks may be maintained across subject areas, giving students the opportunity to see that although their classes may be separated during the school day, the knowledge they gain is connected. Templates for the STEM Research Notebook pages for this module are included in Appendix A.

Emphasize to students the importance of organizing all information in a Research Notebook. Explain to them that scientists and other researchers maintain detailed Research Notebooks in their work. These notebooks, which are crucial to researchers' work because they contain critical information and track the researchers' progress, are often considered legal documents for scientists who are pursuing patents or wish to provide proof of their discovery process.

MODULE LAUNCH

Introduce the concepts of environment, habitat, and needs of living things in a class discussion. Following agreed-upon rules for discussions, ask students these questions:

- What is the environment?

- What are habitats?

- Are there different types of habitats? What kinds of habitats are there?

Then, have students observe various animals and habitats by watching the video "This Land is Your Land" at https://www.youtube.com/watch?v=3C4iRf9gOdY After the video, hold a class discussion about the animals and habitats students saw in the video.

Table 3.1. Prerequisite Key Knowledge and Examples of Applications and Differentiation Strategies

Prerequisite Key Knowledge	Application of Knowledge by Students	Differentiation for Students Needing Knowledge
Science: • Cause and effect	Science: • Determine how the environment, weather, and local animal habitats interact.	Science: • Read aloud picture books to the class and have students identify cause and effect sequences. • Create a class T-chart to record causes and related effects students observe in the classroom, outdoors, and in literature.
Mathematics: • Number sense	Mathematics: • Record temperatures. • Count objects observed during observations. • Record observation data. • Count items recycled.	Mathematics: • Read aloud nonfiction texts about temperature and measurement to the class. • Provide opportunities for students to practice counting observed objects in a variety of settings (e.g., in the classroom and outdoors) and recording numbers of objects observed.
Language and Inquiry Skills: • Make predictions • Create text using words and pictures • Ask and answer questions	Language and Inquiry Skills: • Make a prediction, and then confirm or reject their predictions in scientific investigations. • Share their ideas and record data in STEM Research Notebooks as they engage in environmental investigations. • Develop a school newsletter or blog that reports information about the environment.	Language and Inquiry Skills: • As a class, make predictions when reading fictional texts. • Model the process of using information and prior knowledge to make predictions. • Provide samples of notebook entries. • Provide samples of newsletters and blogs.

POTENTIAL STEM MISCONCEPTIONS

Students enter the classroom with a wide variety of prior knowledge and ideas, so it is important to be alert to misconceptions, or inappropriate understandings of foundational knowledge. These misconceptions can be classified as one of several types: "preconceived notions," opinions based on popular beliefs or understandings; "nonscientific beliefs," knowledge students have gained about science from sources outside the scientific community; "conceptual misunderstandings," incorrect conceptual models based on incomplete understanding of concepts; "vernacular misconceptions," misunderstandings of words based on their common use versus their scientific use; and "factual misconceptions," incorrect or imprecise knowledge learned in early life that remains unchallenged (NRC 1997, p. 28). Misconceptions must be addressed and dismantled in order for students to reconstruct their knowledge, and therefore teachers should be prepared to take the following steps:

- *Identify students' misconceptions.*

- *Provide a forum for students to confront their misconceptions.*

- *Help students reconstruct and internalize their knowledge, based on scientific models. (NRC 1997, p. 29)*

Keeley and Harrington (2010) recommend using diagnostic tools such as probes and formative assessment to identify and confront student misconceptions and begin the process of reconstructing student knowledge. Keeley and Harrington's *Uncovering Student Ideas in Science* series contains probes targeted toward uncovering student misconceptions in a variety of areas and may be a useful resource for addressing student misconceptions in this module.

Some commonly held misconceptions specific to lesson content are provided with each lesson so that you can be alert for student misunderstanding of the science concepts presented and used during this module. The American Association for the Advancement of Science has also identified misconceptions that students frequently hold regarding various science concepts (see the links at *http://assessment.aaas.org/topics*).

SRL PROCESS COMPONENTS

Table 3.2 illustrates some of the activities in the Our Changing Environment module and how they align to the SRL processes before, during, and after learning.

Table 3.2. SRL Learning Components

Learning Process Components	Example from Our Changing Environment	Lesson number and Learning Component
Before Learning		
Motivates students	Students will participate in a litter sorting activity that prompts them to consider what happens to solid waste materials.	Lesson 1, Introductory activity/ Engagement
Evokes prior learning	Students will use their prior knowledge to predict how plants will grow under varying conditions.	Lesson 1, Activity/Exploration
During Learning		**During Learning**
Focuses on important features	Student teams devise designs for a water filtration device using a given set of materials.	Lesson 2, Introductory Activity/ Engagement
Helps students monitor their progress	Students take walking tours of the school neighborhood, recording their observations; the teacher provides feedback on students' observations recorded in their STEM Research Notebook entries.	Lesson 2, Activity/Exploration
After Learning		**After Learning**
Evaluates learning	Students create and present a school newsletter or blog to be distributed to other kindergarten classes and the school to report on how humans have impacted and can impact the environment in the school neighborhood.	Lesson 3, Activity/Exploration
Takes account of what worked and what did not work	Student teams test the toys they designed in the Trash to Toys design challenge and make improvements based on the results of tests.	Lesson 2, Elaboration/Application of Knowledge

STRATEGIES FOR DIFFERENTIATING INSTRUCTION WITHIN THIS MODULE

For the purposes of this curriculum module, differentiated instruction is conceptualized as a way to tailor instruction – including process, content, and product – to various student needs in your class. A number of differentiation strategies are integrated into lessons across the module. The problem- and project-based learning approach used in the lessons is designed to address students' multiple intelligences by providing a variety of entry points and methods to investigate the key concepts in the module (for example, investigating the local environment from the perspectives of science and social issues via scientific inquiry, literature, journaling, and collaborative design). Differentiation strategies for students needing support in prerequisite knowledge can be found in Table 3.1 (p. 28). You are encouraged to use information gained about student prior knowledge during introductory activities and discussions to inform your instructional differentiation. Strategies incorporated into this lesson include flexible grouping, varied environmental learning contexts, assessments, compacting, tiered assignments and scaffolding, and mentoring. The following websites may be helpful resources for differentiated instruction:

- *http://steinhardt.nyu.edu/scmsAdmin/uploads/005/120/Culturally%20Responsive%20 Differentiated%20Instruction.pdf*

- *http://educationnorthwest.org/sites/default/files/12.99.pdf*

Flexible Grouping: Students work collaboratively in a variety of activities throughout this module. Grouping strategies you might employ include student-led grouping, grouping students according to ability level or common interests, grouping students randomly, or grouping them so that students in each group have complementary strengths (for instance, one student might be strong in mathematics, another in art, and another in writing).

Varied Environmental Learning Contexts: Students have the opportunity to learn in various contexts throughout the module, including alone, in groups, in quiet reading and research-oriented activities, and in active learning through inquiry and design activities. In addition, students learn in a variety of ways, including through doing inquiry activities, journaling, reading a variety of texts, watching videos, participating in class discussion, and conducting web-based research.

Assessments: Students are assessed in a variety of ways throughout the module, including individual and collaborative formative and summative assessments. Students have the opportunity to produce work via written text, oral presentations, and modeling.

Compacting: Based on student prior knowledge, you may wish to adjust instructional activities for students who exhibit prior mastery of a learning objective. Since

student work in science and ELA is largely collaborative throughout the module, this strategy may be most appropriate for mathematics or social studies activities.

Tiered Assignments and Scaffolding: Based on your awareness of student ability, understanding of concepts, and mastery of skills, you may wish to provide students with variations on activities by adding complexity to assignments or providing more or fewer learning supports for activities throughout the module. For instance, some students may benefit from cloze sentence handouts to enhance vocabulary understanding. Other students may benefit from expanded reading selections and additional reflective writing or from working with manipulatives and other visual representations of mathematical concepts. You may also work with your school librarian to compile a classroom database of research resources and supplementary readings for different reading levels and on a variety of topics related to the module challenge to provide opportunities for students to undertake independent reading. You may find the following website on scaffolding strategies helpful: *www.edutopia.org/blog/scaffolding-lessons-six-strategies-rebecca-alber.*

Mentoring: As group design teamwork becomes increasingly complex throughout the module, you may wish to have a resource teacher, older student, or volunteer work with groups that struggle to stay on task and collaborate effectively.

STRATEGIES FOR ENGLISH LANGUAGE LEARNERS (ELLS)

Students who are developing proficiency in English language skills require additional supports to simultaneously learn academic content and the specialized language associated with specific content areas. WIDA has created a framework for providing support to these students and makes available rubrics and guidance on differentiating instructional materials for English language learners (ELLs) (see *https://wida.wisc.edu*). In particular, ELL students may benefit from additional sensory supports such as images, physical modeling, and graphic representations of module content, as well as interactive support through collaborative work. This module incorporates a variety of sensory supports and offers ongoing opportunities for ELL students to work with collaboratively.

Teachers differentiating instruction for ELL students should carefully consider the needs of these students as they introduce and use academic language in various language domains (listening, speaking, reading, and writing) throughout this module. To adequately differentiate instruction for ELL students, teachers should have an understanding of the proficiency level of each student. The following five overarching PreK–5 WIDA learning standards are relevant to this module:

> Standard 1: Social and Instructional Language. Focus on following directions, personal information, collaboration with peers.

Standard 2: The language of Language Arts. Focus on non-fiction, fiction, sequence of story, elements of story.

Standard 3: The language of Mathematics. Focus on basic operations, number sense, interpretation of data, patterns.

Standard 4: The language of Science. Focus on forces in nature, scientific process, living and nonliving things, organisms and environment.

Standard 5: The language of Social Studies. Focus homes and habitats, jobs and careers, geography, representations of Earth (maps and globes).

SAFETY CONSIDERATIONS FOR THE ACTIVITIES IN THIS MODULE

Student activities in this module focus on observing various natural phenomena, including growing plants, and handling recyclable materials. Students should use caution when handling scissors, bottles, and cans. Sharp points or edges can cut or puncture skin, and bottles can break if not handled carefully. Also caution students not to eat seeds, as they may be treated with toxic chemicals. For more general safety guidelines, see the Safety in STEM section in Chapter 2 (pp. 18–19).

DESIRED OUTCOMES AND MONITORING SUCCESS

The desired outcomes for this module are outlined in Table 3.3, along with suggested ways to gather evidence to monitor student success. For more specific details on desired outcomes, see the Established Goals and Objectives sections for the module and individual lessons.

Table 3.3. Desired Outcomes and Evidence of Success in Achieving Identified Outcomes

Desired Outcome	Evidence of Success	
	Performance Tasks	Other Measures
Students understand and can demonstrate human interactions with and impact on the environment, including the localized effects of pollution and the effects of weather changes on local animal habitats.	• Student teams conduct environmental investigations to explore the environment in the school neighborhood. • Student teams use the EDP to repurpose waste materials in the Toys to Trash Design Challenge activity. • The class will produce a newsletter or blog conveying information about the school community.	Students are assessed using the Observation, STEM Research Notebook, and Participation Rubric.

Lesson	Assessment	Group/ Individual	Formative/ Summative	Lesson Objective Assessed
1	Environment Drawing and Description *end of lesson assessment*	Individual	Formative	• Define environment
2	STEM Research Notebook *entries*	Individual	Summative	• Define pollution • Describe how pollution affects the environment, habitats, and all living things
2	STEM Research Notebook *prompts*	Group/ Individual	Formative	• Describe several ways that human activity causes pollution • Describe several ways that people can prevent pollution or clean up the effects of pollution
2	Participation in class weather observations and analysis *observation and participation rubric*	Individual	Formative	• Understand local weather patterns and be able to make connections between the weather and local environmental conditions
2	Our Neighborhood Environmental Health Walking Tour *performance task*	Group	Formative	• Describe how pollution affects the environment, habitats, and all living things • Identify and describe living (animals, insects, and plants) components of their school neighborhood • Identify features of their school neighborhood that can be smelled and heard
2	Trash to Toys Design Challenge *products and presentations*	Group	Formative	• Describe the EDP as the process engineers use to solve problems • Understand the influence of recycling of materials used in consumer products on the environment • Use the EDP to turn waste items into toys
2	Pollution Drawing and Description *end of lesson assessment*	Individual	Summative	• Define pollution • Describe how pollution affects the environment, habitats, and all living things
3	STEM Research Notebook *entries*	Group/ Individual	Formative	• Describe the local environment using text and illustrations • Communicate to others via text and illustrations the impacts humans can have on the environment • Communicate to others via text and illustrations ways that humans can care for the environment

Continued

Table 3.5. (*continued*)

Lesson	Assessment	Group/ Individual	Formative/ Summative	Lesson Objective Assessed
3	Participation in class weather observations and analysis *observation and participation rubric*	Individual	Formative	• Understand local weather patterns and be able to make connections between the weather and local environmental conditions
3	Good Neighbors Class Project *performance task*	Group	Summative	• Create and implement a plan to positively impact the local environment
3	Class Newsletter or Blog *performance task*	Group	Summative	• Describe the local environment using text and illustrations • Communicate to others via text and illustrations the impacts humans can have on the environment • Communicate to others via text and illustrations ways that humans can care for the environment • Design and produce a class newsletter or blog to report findings about the local environment
3	Caring for Environment Drawing and Description *end of lesson assessment*	Individual	Summative	• Communicate to others via text and illustrations the impacts humans can have on the environment • Communicate to others via text and illustrations ways that humans can care for the environment

MODULE TIMELINE

Tables 3.6–3.10 provide lesson timelines for each week of the module. These timelines are provided for general guidance only and are based on class times of approximately 30 minutes.

Table 3.6. STEM Road Map Module Schedule Week One

Day 1	Day 2	Day 3	Day 4	Day 5
Lesson 1 *Our Amazing Environment!* Launch the module. Group discussion on environment, habitats, and basic needs of living things. Introduce weather chart. Introduce classroom recycling program with the Litter Bits Activity.	*Lesson 1* *Our Amazing Environment!* Students participate in a kinesthetic activity to demonstrate plant growth. Conduct an interactive read aloud – *Red Leaf, Yellow Leaf* by Lois Ehlert.	*Lesson 1* *Our Amazing Environment!* Conduct an interactive read aloud – *Recycle That!* by Fay Robinson. Begin Super Sunflowers investigation (Predict).	*Lesson 1* *Our Amazing Environment!* Continue Super Sunflowers investigation (plant seeds – ongoing observation throughout the module).	*Lesson 1* *Our Amazing Environment!* Introduce module challenge. Assessment.

Table 3.7. STEM Road Map Module Schedule Week Two

Day 6	Day 7	Day 8	Day 9	Day 10
Lesson 2 *Let's Explore Our Neighborhood Environment!* Introduce pollution by a class discussion. Introduce water pollution. Conduct an interactive read aloud – *Water Pollution* by Rhonda Lucas Donald.	*Lesson 2* *Let's Explore Our Neighborhood Environment!* Conduct the water filter design class activity.	*Lesson 2* *Let's Explore Our Neighborhood Environment!* Watch video about water pollution. Introduce Our Neighborhood Environmental Health investigation.	*Lesson 2* *Let's Explore Our Neighborhood Environment!* Continue Our Neighborhood Environmental Health investigation.	*Lesson 2* *Let's Explore Our Neighborhood Environment!* Continue Our Neighborhood Environmental Health investigation.

Table 3.8. STEM Road Map Module Schedule Week Three

Day 11	Day 12	Day 13	Day 14	Day 15
Lesson 2 *Let's Explore Our Neighborhood Environment!* Introduce air pollution interactive read aloud – *Air Pollution* by Rhonda Lucas Donald Continue Our Neighborhood Environmental Health investigation.	*Lesson 2* *Let's Explore Our Neighborhood Environment!* Continue Our Neighborhood Environmental Health investigation.	*Lesson 2* *Let's Explore Our Neighborhood Environment!* Introduce Trash to Toys Design Challenge activity with interactive read aloud – *One Plastic Bag: Isatou Ceesay and the Recycling Women of Gambia* by Miranda Paul and Elizabeth Zunon	*Lesson 2* *Let's Explore Our Neighborhood Environment!* Introduce EDP	*Lesson 2* *Let's Explore Our Neighborhood Environment!* Begin Trash to Toys Design Challenge activity.

Table 3.9. STEM Road Map Module Schedule Week Four

Day 16	Day 17	Day 18	Day 19	Day 20
Lesson 2 *Let's Explore Our Neighborhood Environment!* Continue Trash to Toys Design Challenge activity.	*Lesson 2* *Let's Explore Our Neighborhood Environment!* Conclude Trash to Toys Design Challenge activity. Students share toy designs with class.	*Lesson 3* *Neighborhood News* Review module challenge. View video "Change the World in 5 Minutes."	*Lesson 3* *Neighborhood News* Introduce Good Neighbors class project. Students brainstorm ideas for ways they can care for the neighborhood environment. Interactive read aloud – *Cleaning up Litter* by Charlotte Guillan or *Look Out for Litter* by Lisa Bullard.	*Lesson 3* *Neighborhood News* Continue Good Neighbors class project (implement project). View video about planting trees.

Table 3.10. STEM Road Map Module Schedule Week Five

Day 21	Day 22	Day 23	Day 24	Day 25
Lesson 3 *Neighborhood News* Students collect information for newsletter or blog by completing My Environment News template.	*Lesson 3* *Neighborhood News* Students collect information for newsletter or blog by completing My Environment News template.	*Lesson 3* *Neighborhood News* Students make final decisions about newsletter/blog. Begin to create newsletter/blog.	*Lesson 3* *Neighborhood News* Create newsletter/blog.	*Lesson 3* *Neighborhood News* Complete newsletter/blog. Assessment.

RESOURCES

The media specialist can help teachers locate resources for students to view and read about habitats, plants and animals native to the local environment, weather, and related content. Special educators and reading specialists can help identify supplemental sources for students needing extra support in reading and writing. Additional resources may be found online. Community resources for this module may include naturalists, biologists, and representatives from environmental and recycling organizations such as the county or township recycling coordinator and the local environmental commission.

REFERENCES

Keeley, P., and R. Harrington. 2010. *Uncovering student ideas in physical science, volume 1: 45 new force and motion assessment probes*. Arlington, VA: NSTA Press.

Koehler, C., M. A. Bloom, and A. R. Milner. 2015. The STEM Road Map for grades K–2. In *STEM Road Map: A framework for integrated STEM education*, ed. C. C. Johnson, E. E. Peters-Burton, and T. J. Moore, 41–67. New York: Routledge. *www.routledge.com/products/9781138804234*.

National Research Council (NRC). 1997. *Science teaching reconsidered: A handbook*. Washington, DC: National Academies Press.

WIDA. 2012. 2012 Amplification of the English language development standards: Kindergarten – Grade 12. *https://wida.wisc.edu/sites/default/files/resource/2012-ELD-Standards.pdf*.

OUR CHANGING ENVIRONMENT LESSON PLANS

Vanessa B. Morrison, Andrea R. Milner, Janet B. Walton,
Carla C. Johnson, and Erin E. Peters-Burton

Lesson Plan 1:
Our Amazing Environment!

In this lesson, students will explore the environment, various habitats, and the basic needs of living things through an investigation of plant growing conditions in the Super Sunflowers investigation.

ESSENTIAL QUESTIONS

- What is the environment?

- What are habitats?

- What are different types of habitats?

- What are the basic needs of all living things? (air, water, food, shelter, and sunlight)

- What do you think happens when the basic needs of living things are not met?

ESTABLISHED GOALS AND OBJECTIVES

At the conclusion of this lesson, students will be able to do the following:

- Define environment

- Define habitat and identify several types of habitats

- Identify the basic needs of all living things as air, water, food, shelter, and sunlight

DOI: 10.4324/9781003261728-6

- Understand and describe the basic components of the life cycle of plants

- Chart, graph, identify, describe, and analyze patterns of local weather to make connections between weather and conditions in the local environment

- Identify and demonstrate recycling practices, including sorting materials and tracking amounts of materials recycled

TIME REQUIRED

5 days (approximately 30 minutes each; see Table 3.6, p. 37)

MATERIALS

Required Materials for Lesson 1

- STEM Research Notebooks (1 per student, see pp. 12–13 for STEM Research Notebook information)

- Computer with internet access for viewing videos

- iPads, smartphones, or tablets for student videotaping (optional)

- Weather chart for the entire class (create or purchase) or handouts for each student (attached at the end of this lesson)

- Images of various types of habitats (e.g., a desert, a marsh, a suburban backyard)

- Crayons for use in STEM Research Notebook entries (1 set per student)

- Chart paper

- Markers

- Map and/or globe

- 2 spray bottles – 1 filled with water and 1 empty (1 set per class)

- Flashlight (1 per class)

- Safety glasses or goggles, nonlatex aprons, and nonlatex gloves

- Books

  o *Recycle That!* by Fay Robinson

  o *Red Leaf, Yellow Leaf* by Lois Ehlert

Additional Materials for Litter Bits Activity

Assortment of plastic items for demonstration, some with recycling symbol and some without

Per team of 3–4 students:

- 2 boxes (for example copier paper boxes, about 15"x12"x10") OR 2 plastic garbage bags

- 1 garbage bag filled with an assortment of items that are trash and items that are recyclable (e.g., paper, cardboard, plastic, empty milk cartons, food waste sealed inside plastic bags, string, plastic bags, empty cans with no sharp edges)

Additional Materials for Super Sunflowers Investigation (per team of 2 students)

- The bottom half of 3 clear 2-liter bottles (see Lesson Preparation, pp. 52–54)

- Scissors

- Tape

- 3 Plastic plates

- 5 cups of potting soil

- 6 sunflower seeds

- Masking tape

- Permanent marker

- Plastic cup (16 ounce size)

- Access to water (about 12 ounces)

- Rulers (for ongoing observations)

SAFETY NOTES

1. Remind students that personal protective equipment (safety glasses or goggles, aprons, and gloves) must be worn during the setup, hands-on, and take-down segments of the activity.

2. Caution students not to eat seeds, which may have been treated with toxic chemicals such as herbicides, pesticides, or fungicides.

3. Students should use caution when handling scissors, as the sharp points and blades can cut or puncture skin.

4. Immediately wipe up any spilled water or soil on the floor to avoid a slip-and-fall hazard.

5. Have students wash hands with soap and water after the activity is completed.

CONTENT STANDARDS AND KEY VOCABULARY

Table 4.1 lists the content standards from the *Next Generation Science Standards (NGSS)*, *Common Core State Standards (CCSS)*, National Association for the Education of Young Children (NAEYC), and the Framework for 21st Century Learning that this lesson addresses, and Table 4.2 (pp. 47–48) presents the key vocabulary. Vocabulary terms are provided for both teacher and student use. Teachers may choose to introduce some or all of the terms to students.

Table 4.1. Standards Addressed in STEM Road Map Module Lesson One

---

NEXT GENERATION SCIENCE STANDARDS

PERFORMANCE EXPECTATIONS

- K-LS1-1. Use observations to describe patterns of what plants and animals (including humans) need to survive.

- K-ESS2-1. Use and share observations of local weather conditions to describe patterns over time.

- K-ESS2-2. Construct an argument supported by evidence for how plants and animals (including humans) can change the environment to meet their needs.

- K-PS3-1. Make observations to determine the effect of sunlight on Earth's surface.

SCIENCE AND ENGINEERING PRACTICES

Analyzing and Interpreting Data

- Analyzing data in K-2 builds on prior experiences and progresses to collecting, recording, and sharing observations.

- Use observations (firsthand or from media) to describe patterns in the natural world in order to answer scientific questions.

Planning and Carrying Out Investigations

- Planning and carrying out investigations to answer questions or test solutions to problems in K-2 builds on prior experiences and progresses to simple investigations, based on fair tests, which provide data to support explanations or design solutions.

- Make observations (firsthand or from media) to collect data that can be used to make comparisons.

DISCIPLINARY CORE IDEAS

LS1.C. *Organization for Matter and Energy Flow in Organisms*

- All animals need food in order to live and grow. They obtain their food from plants or from other animals. Plants need water and light to live and grow.

ESS3.A. *Natural Resources*

• Living things need water, air, and resources from the land, and they live in places that have the things they need. Humans use natural resources for everything they do.

PS3.B. *Conservation of Energy and Energy Transfer*

• Sunlight warms Earth's surface.

CROSSCUTTING CONCEPTS

Patterns

• Patterns in the natural and human designed world can be observed and used as evidence.

Systems and System Models

• Systems in the natural and designed world have parts that work together.

Cause and Effect

• Events have causes that generate observable patterns.

COMMON CORE STATE STANDARDS FOR MATHEMATICS
MATHEMATICAL PRACTICES

• MP1. Make sense of problems and persevere in solving them.

• MP2. Reason abstractly and quantitatively.

• MP3. Construct viable arguments and critique the reasoning of others.

• MP4. Model with mathematics.

• MP5. Use appropriate tools strategically.

• MP6. Attend to precision.

• MP7. Look for and make use of structure.

• MP8. Look for and express regularity in repeated reasoning.

MATHEMATICAL CONTENT

• K.CC.B.4. Understand the relationship between numbers and quantities; connect counting to cardinality.

• K.CC.B.4a. When counting objects, say the number names in the standard order, pairing each object with one and only one number name and each number name with one and only one object.

• K.CC.B.4b. Understand that the last number name said tells the number of objects counted. The number of objects is the same regardless of their arrangement or the order in which they were counted.

Continued

Table 4.1. (*continued*)

- K.CC.B.4c. Understand that each successive number name refers to a quantity that is one larger.
- K.CC.C.6. Identify whether the number of objects in one group is greater than, less than, or equal to the number of objects in another group, e.g., by using matching and counting strategies.
- K.CC.C.7. Compare two numbers between 1 and 10 presented as written numerals.
- K.MD.A.1. Describe measurable attributes of objects, such as length or weight. Describe several measurable attributes of a single object.
- K.MD.A.2. Directly compare two objects with a measurable attribute in common, to see which object has "more of"/"less of" the attribute, and describe the difference. For example, directly compare the heights of two children and describe one child as taller/shorter.
- K.MD.B.3. Classify objects into given categories; count the numbers of objects in each category and sort the categories by count.

COMMON CORE STATE STANDARDS FOR ENGLISH LANGUAGE ARTS
READING STANDARDS

- RI.K.1. With prompting and support, ask and answer questions about key details in a text.
- RI.K.3. With prompting and support, describe the connection between two individuals, events, ideas, or pieces of information in a text.

WRITING STANDARDS

- W.K.2 Use a combination of drawing, dictating, and writing to compose informative/explanatory texts in which they name what they are writing about and supply some information about the topic.
- W.K.5 With guidance and support from adults, respond to questions and suggestions from peers and add details to strengthen writing as needed.
- W.K.7 Participate in shared research and writing projects (e.g., explore a number of books by a favorite author and express opinions about them).

SPEAKING AND LISTENING STANDARDS

- SL.K.1. Participate in collaborative conversations with diverse partners about kindergarten topics and texts with peers and adults in small and larger groups.
- SL.K.3. Ask and answer questions in order to seek help, get information, or clarify something that is not understood.
- SL.K.5. Add drawings or other visual displays to descriptions as desired to provide additional detail.

NATIONAL ASSOCIATION FOR THE EDUCATION OF YOUNG CHILDREN STANDARDS

2.G.02. Children are provided varied opportunities and materials to learn key content and principles of science.

2.G.03. Children are provided with varied opportunities and materials that encourage them to use the five senses to observe, explore, and experiment with scientific phenomena.

2.G.04. Children are provided with varied opportunities to use simple tools to observe objects and scientific phenomena.

2.G.05. Children are provided with varied opportunities and materials to collect data and to represent and document their findings (e.g., through drawing or graphing).

2.G.06. Children are provided with varied opportunities and materials that encourage them to think, question, and reason about observed and inferred phenomena.

2.G.07. Children are provided with varied opportunities and materials that encourage them to discuss scientific concepts in everyday conversation.

2.G.08. Children are provided with varied opportunities and materials that help them learn and use scientific terminology and vocabulary associated with the content areas.

2.H.02. All children have opportunities to access technology that they can use.

2.H.03. Technology is used to extend learning within the classroom and integrate and enrich the curriculum.

FRAMEWORK FOR 21ST CENTURY LEARNING

Interdisciplinary Themes; Learning and Innovation Skills; Information, Media and Technology Skills; Life and Career Skills

Table 4.2. Key Vocabulary for Lesson 1

Key Vocabulary	Definition
climate	the weather conditions in an area over an extended period of time
drought	a long period of dry weather with very little rainfall
Earth	the planet where we live
environment	the conditions and objects including living things that are in our surroundings
garbage	things that are no longer usable and do not get recycled; trash
habitat	a place in nature where plants, animals, and people grow and live

Continued

Table 4.2. (*continued*)

Key Vocabulary	Definition
prevent	to take action to stop something from taking place
pollution	anything that humans add to the environment that is harmful to animals, plants and/or people
recycle	to turn waste into something that can be used again
seasons	four different times of the year, each with different weather conditions; winter, spring, summer, and fall
waste	as a verb, to use something carelessly; as a noun, something that is no longer useful in its present form
weather	the daily conditions over a particular area that includes temperature, precipitation, cloud cover, and wind

TEACHER BACKGROUND INFORMATION

Kindergarteners are rapidly developing across all domains (physical, social and emotional, personality, cognitive, and language) and are able to make connections across multiple content areas (STEM and ELA). They are developing logical thinking skills, the ability to reason out problems, autonomy, and growing independence. Through this module, you should support and facilitate the development of these developmental domains and content areas within each student. For information about how formative assessments can be used to connect student prior experiences with classroom instruction, see the STEM Teaching Tools resource "Making Science Instruction Compelling for All Students: Using Cultural Formative Assessment to Build on Learner Interest and Experience" at *http://stemteachingtools.org/pd/sessionc.*

Habitats

For the purposes of this module, habitat is defined broadly as a place in nature where plants, animals, and people grow and live. Within this module, students will consider large scale habitats such as the ocean, forests, and grasslands, and habitats on a smaller scale including their schoolyards and neighborhoods. Students will extend their understanding of habitats as they learn about the five basic needs of living things - air, water, food, shelter, and sunlight. Throughout the module's activities and discussions, students will arrive at an understanding that habitats are the diverse environments in which living things have their basic needs met.

Environmental Changes and Weather Patterns

This module focuses on environmental changes at a level observable to kindergarten students. Students should understand that humans can impact the environment and other living creatures by polluting the air and water, by mismanaging solid waste (littering), and by destroying habitats (clear-cutting forests, etc.). The Environmental Protection Agency (EPA) provides information and resources for educators that you may find helpful. See the EPA's "Learning and Teaching About the Environment" page at *www.epa.gov/students* for more information.

In this module, the class will track daily weather conditions and look for connections between weather and changes they observe in the surrounding environment, including changes due to changes in the seasons. Since students may have heard the term climate, be prepared to distinguish between weather as daily atmospheric conditions in an area and climate as the weather conditions in an area over an extended period of time. You should emphasize to students that the class's observations do not span enough time to reflect climate patterns or changes, since interpreting these patterns requires collecting and analyzing data for many years. For more information on the distinction between weather and climate, see NASA's "What's the difference between weather and climate?" page at *www.nasa.gov/mission_pages/noaa-n/climate/climate_weather.html.*

Career Connections

You may wish to connect students' work in this module with specific careers. For example, Koehler, Bloom, and Milner (2015) suggest connecting the following careers to kindergartners' learning:

- biologist
- botanist
- ecologist
- engineer
- farmer
- geographer
- journalist
- mathematician
- meteorologist
- scientist

For more information about these and other careers, see Bureau of Labor Statistics' *Occupational Outlook Handbook* at *www.bls.gov/ooh/home.html*.

One suggestion for incorporating careers is to hold a career dress-up day. To do this, you should provide a box of props and allow students to dress up as people working in various careers and hold a "fashion show" featuring each student dressed as a person in a career (for example, a botanist might wear a hat and have a magnifying glass and a plant identification book; a journalist might carry a camera and hold a notebook and paper; a farmer might wear a straw hat and a flannel shirt and hold a model tractor).

In this module, students will be introduced to the idea that engineers and other STEM workers work together in teams to solve problems. Students will experience working in teams and in pairs as they progress through a simple scientific process including predicting, observing, and explaining phenomena related to forces in this lesson. This introduction to teamwork sets the stage for students' use of the engineering design process (EDP) later in the module.

Know, Want to Know, Learned (KWL) Charts

Throughout this module, you will track student knowledge on Know, Want to Know, Learned (KWL) charts. These charts will be used to access and assess student prior knowledge, encourage students to think critically about the topic under discussion, and track student learning throughout the module. Each chart should consist of three columns, labeled "What We Know," "What We Want to Know," and "What We Learned." Write the topic at the top of each chart. It may be helpful to post these charts in a prominent place in the classroom so that students can refer to them throughout the module. Students will include their personal know, want to know, and learned reflections in their STEM Research Notebooks entries.

Interactive Read-Alouds

This module also uses interactive read-alouds to engage students, access their prior knowledge, develop student background knowledge, and introduce topical vocabulary. These read-alouds expose children to teacher-read literature that may be beyond their independent reading levels but is consistent with their listening level. Interactive read-alouds may incorporate a variety of techniques, and you can find helpful information regarding these techniques at the following websites:

- *www.readingrockets.org/article/repeated-interactive-read-alouds-preschool-and-kindergarten*

- *www.k5chalkbox.com/interactive-read-aloud.html*

- *www.readwritethink.org/professional-development/strategy-guides/teacher-read-aloud-that-30799.html*

In general, interactive read-alouds provide opportunities for students to share prior knowledge and experiences, interact with the text and concepts introduced therein, launch conversations about the topics introduced, construct meaning, make predictions, and draw comparisons. You may wish to mark places within the texts to pause to ask for student experiences, predictions, or other ideas. Each reading experience should focus on an ongoing interaction between students and the text, including the following:

- Allow students to share personal stories throughout the reading.

- Ask students to predict throughout the story.

- Allow students to add new ideas from the book to the KWL chart and their STEM Research Notebooks.

- Allow students to add new words from the book to the vocabulary chart and their STEM Research Notebooks.

The materials list for each lesson includes the books for interactive read-alouds that you will use in that lesson. A list of suggested books for additional reading can be found at the end of this chapter (see p. 100).

COMMON MISCONCEPTIONS

Students will have various types of prior knowledge about the concepts introduced in this lesson. Table 4.3 outlines some common misconceptions students may have concerning these concepts. Because of the breadth of students' experiences, it is not possible to anticipate every misconception that students may bring as they approach this lesson. Incorrect or inaccurate prior understanding of concepts can influence student learning in the future, however, so it is important to be alert to misconceptions such as those presented in the table.

Table 4.3. Common Misconceptions About the Concepts in Lesson 1

Topic	Student Misconception	Explanation
Environmental Science	The temperature of the air is the same everywhere on earth.	Air temperature varies widely in various places on Earth and is affected by factors such as surface temperature, ocean currents, altitude and geographic position, and cloud cover

Continued

Table 4.3. (*continued*)

Topic	Student Misconception	Explanation
Life Science	Different kinds of organisms do not compete with each other for resources such as water. Plants take in everything they need from the Sun and air or, alternatively, plants take in everything they need from their roots.	All living things need food, water, shelter, sunlight and air, and compete with each other for these resources. Plants need sunlight and air to create energy, and they also need the minerals and water they absorb through their roots.
	Plants depend on people for their needs (sunlight, water, and nutrients).	While people may care for plants, especially those kept indoors, plants are primarily dependent on their natural environments for their needs.

PREPARATION FOR LESSON 1

Review the Teacher Background Information, assemble the materials for the lesson, duplicate the student handouts, and preview the videos recommended in the Learning Components section below. Present students with their STEM Research Notebooks and explain how these will be used (see pp. 12–13). Templates for the STEM Research Notebook are provided in Appendix A, and a rubric for observations, student participation, and STEM Research Notebook entries is provided in Appendix B.

STEM Research Notebook entry #2 provides a template for students to record vocabulary words. You may wish to use this template throughout the module for students to record definitions and illustrations of key vocabulary words. The template provides space for definitions and illustrations of three words. If you introduce more than three vocabulary words in a lesson you should make multiple copies of the template for each student.

Students will track the local weather throughout the module. Create or purchase a weather chart for class use that will accommodate your needs based on your local weather patterns. A sample of weather symbols is provided at the end of this lesson. You may also wish to have students track the weather conditions individually; a sample weather chart is provided at the end of this lesson. You should adjust the weather-tracking methods to your region and the time of year. For example, if you live in an area where the weather is consistently warm, you may wish to focus on daily weather patterns, such as the change in temperature over the day and changes in the amount of cloud cover each day. Alternatively, if you are using this module in a place and during a time period in which seasonal weather changes are occurring, you may wish to focus on weekly trends, such as the number of days with a high temperature over 70 degrees each week.

You may wish to create a "weather window" as a cue to students to observe the weather and to help them focus their attention on weather conditions. To do this, create a cardboard frame with an opening that is about 16" x 20" and with a frame width of about three inches. You may decorate the frame with weather symbols (e.g., cloud, sun, raindrop cutouts). Either secure the frame to a classroom window through which students will observe daily weather conditions or be prepared to manually place the frame against the window and ask students to look through it as they make their daily weather observations.

Students will also participate in a classroom recycling program during this module. How you structure this program will depend on available space and the recycling resources in your community. One option is for students to recycle cans for money (if this is available in your area) and donate the funds to a local zoo, nature center, or other conservation organization. In this case, you may wish to have students bring clean aluminum cans from home to contribute to the recycling program. Alternatively, you may wish to have students recycle classroom waste or waste from their lunches. Another option is to have students collect paper or plastic waste from other classrooms to include in the class recycling effort. Familiarize yourself with what materials can be recycled in your area and how the materials can be collected from your school and delivered to a recycling facility or, if your school recycles, included with the school's recycling. Prepare a space with labeled bins for students to sort and count recyclables and a place to store them until they can be delivered to a recycling center. You should also prepare a chart to track daily recycling (e.g., number of items, types of items).

For the Litter Bits activity, label one box or bag for each team "Recycle" and one "Trash." Assemble an assortment of recyclable items and trash items for each team and place them in a bag. Assemble several plastic items, some with a recycling symbol, some without.

Students will plant sunflower seeds for an ongoing investigation, Super Sunflowers, in which they observe plant growth under varying conditions of water and light. This activity requires that each team of 2–3 students have three clear 2-liter bottles, cut in half with 3–4 small drainage holes in the bottom. You should prepare these bottles in advance. You will need to provide space in a sunny location for two bottles from each team. The third bottle from each team will be placed in a location out of the sun. Care instructions for each of the three bottles is provided in the Activity/Investigation section. You should plan to have the students care for the seeds as instructed for the remainder of the module. If seeds have not germinated within thirteen days it is unlikely that they will, so you may conclude at that point that the seeds will not grow. Be sure to survey conditions in your classroom for additional factors that may affect plant growth, such as heaters or air conditioning units, and try to situate the plants in an area where they will not affect the plants.

Zoo or nature center displays are an excellent way to demonstrate animal habitats and how animals live together. An option for the module is to schedule a zoo or nature

center field trip as an opportunity for students to experience animal habitats first-hand. If you choose to do this, you should begin making appropriate plans.

LEARNING COMPONENTS
Introductory Activity/Engagement

Connection to the Challenge: Begin each day of this lesson by directing students' attention to the module challenge, the Environmental Explorers Challenge:

> *Your class has been challenged to teach other students at your school about the plant and animal habitats in your area, and ways that they can care for the environment to protect these habitats and make sure that your town's environment is clean and healthy for people as well as other animals and plants.*

Remind students of the driving question for the module: How can we care for the environment?

Tell students that they will create a web log or newsletter for other students at their school. To do this, they will need to learn about habitats in your area, what plants need to grow, and how people can care for the environment. On each day of the lesson, hold a brief class discussion of how students' learning in the previous days' lessons contributed to their ability to complete the challenge. You may wish to create a class list of key ideas on chart paper.

ELA and Science Classes: Introduce the concepts of environment, habitat, and needs of living things in a class discussion. Following agreed-upon rules for discussions, ask students these questions:

- What is the environment?

- What are habitats? (Introduce the definition of habitat as a place in nature where plants, animals, and people grow and live)

- Are there different types of habitats? What kinds of habitats are there?

Then, have students observe various animals and habitats in the U.S. by watching the video "This Land is Your Land" at *www.youtube.com/watch?v=3C4iRf9gOdY*. After the video, hold a class discussion about the animals and habitats students saw in the video. As students name animals, ask students to describe with words how the animal moves through its habitat (e.g., crawling, slithering, hopping), and make a list of the animals and the habitat in which students observed each animal on chart paper. Next, have students move to an open area and call out various animals from the class list. As you call out an animal's name, have students perform the action they described for that animal. At the conclusion of each action, have the class repeat together a statement about how the animal moves through its habitat (e.g., "rabbits move through a meadow by hopping," "snakes move through a desert by slithering," or "fish move through the water by swimming").

Next, choose a student to act out one of the animal motions from the class chart and instruct the rest of the class to name the animal and the habitat by again making a statement about how the animal moves through its habitat. Repeat, choosing different students to act out motions, until all motions from the class list have been represented. Point out to students that sometimes animals that use similar motions can live in different habitats (e.g., frogs and kangaroos both hop, but a frog may live in a swamp and a kangaroo in a grassy plain).

STEM Research Notebook Entry #1

Have students draw and label two different habitats they have seen or that they saw in the video (for example, forest, prairie, desert, ocean, mountain).

Focus students' attention on the term *environment* and emphasize to them that weather is an important part of the environment in which they live and in which plants live. Begin a class vocabulary chart including words and pictures. You should post the chart on classroom wall for student reference throughout the module. Add vocabulary as necessary and consistently refer to the chart and module vocabulary. Students will create a STEM Research Notebook entry recording vocabulary.

STEM Research Notebook Entry #2

Have students add vocabulary words in their STEM Research Notebooks using words and pictures. Words to include are environment, weather, and habitat.

Introduce students to the weather chart that the class will maintain throughout the module. Ask students for their ideas about why understanding weather might be useful for understanding habitats and the environment (e.g., knowing what the weather conditions are like will help them understand when animals need to begin to store food for the winter). If you chose to create a weather window frame, hold the frame up to a window and ask students to look through it and describe what they observe. Beginning on Day 1, at the start of every class, students will observe and chart, graph, identify, describe, and analyze patterns of local weather to make connections among daily weather and what they observe in the environment. These observations will be made throughout the module to enable students to relate weather to changes in habitats. Working as a class, students should observe and chart the following daily:

- whether each day is warmer than, colder than, or the same temperature as the previous day

- descriptions of the weather (such as sunny, cloudy, rainy, and warm)

- numbers of sunny, windy, and rainy days in a month

Mathematics and Social Studies Connections: Introduce the class recycling program by asking students for their ideas about what happens to their garbage after they put it into a trash can. Guide students to understand that the accumulation of solid waste in landfills is one type of pollution that can affect the environment. Ask students to share their ideas about how solid waste pollution can affect the environment. Introduce the idea that recycling reduces the amount of solid waste in landfills. Students will begin a recycling program in the classroom to help facilitate a healthy environment, making the connection that recycling and disposing of waste properly can reduce pollution. Introduce the concept of recycling by asking students what recycling is and how it is related to the environment. Students will explore the concept of recycling through an interactive read aloud of *Recycle That!* by Fay Robinson. Students will create STEM Research Notebook entries after the reading. You should also track student responses on a KWL chart.

STEM Research Notebook Entry #3

Have students document what they learned about recycling in their STEM Research Notebooks, using both words and pictures.

On a daily basis, students should sort, count, chart, and graph (e.g., number of items, types of items) the recyclables collected and compare daily totals. If your area has a paid recycling program and you will be donating funds, make a chart to tally the total amount of money donated throughout the school year. Students will prepare for the class recycling program in the Litter Bits activity.

Litter Bits

Tell students that they will be sorting recyclable materials each day of the module, but that they need to be able to recognize what items are recyclable and what items are trash. Ask students to share their ideas of items that can be recycled and those that cannot. Next, show students some of the plastic items you assembled and ask students if these are recyclable. Show students how to look for the recycling symbol to tell if an item is recyclable and explain that some plastic items are recyclable and some are not. Ask students to name other items that can be recycled that may not have a recycling symbol (paper, cardboard, aluminum cans). Make a class chart with two columns label "Recyclable" and "Trash" and add the items students identified as recyclable to the "Recyclable" column along. Next, ask students to name items that are not recyclable (e.g., plastics without a recycling symbol, food waste, household items such as broken plates) and add items to the column of the chart labeled "Trash." Review the two columns with students.

Group students in teams of 3–4. Give each team one box or bag labeled "Recycle" and one box or bag labeled "Trash" and point out the labels to them, reminding them that the box or bag with the label that begins with "R" (demonstrate the R sound) is for recyclable materials and the box or bag with the label that begins with "T" (demonstrate the T sound) is for trash. Next, give each team a bag full of the recyclable and non-recyclable materials you assembled. Tell students that some items in the bag are recyclable and some are trash, and that their challenge is to sort everything in the bag into one of the labeled boxes or bags. After students have completed their sorting, have each team count the number of recyclable items and the number of trash items they had and record the numbers on a class chart, asking each team to report whether they had more recyclable items or more trash items.

Activity/Exploration

ELA and Science Classes: Introduce students to plant growth and life cycles through an interactive read aloud of *Red Leaf, Yellow Leaf* by Lois Ehlert. Students will create STEM Research Notebook entries after the reading and the following activity. You should also document student ideas on a KWL chart.

Next, have students participate in a kinesthetic activity in which they act out plant growth. Have students move to an open area. Demonstrate to students how a seed sprouts by kneeling on the floor with your head down and then slowly arising to your knees with your arms at your sides. Tell students that they are going to act as sprouting seeds also but remind them that seeds have needs that must be met before they sprout. Ask students for their ideas about what seeds need to sprout (food from the soil and water).

Have students kneel on the floor with their heads down, acting as "plant seeds." Remind students that the seed needs food from the soil. Have the students pretend to pick up food from the surrounding area (the soil) to eat, reminding students that they are pretending to eat and cautioning them not to put anything in their mouths. Ask them if this is enough for them to sprout (no, the seeds also need water and light). Using a spray bottle, spritz the air above the students, and prompt them to "sprout" as you demonstrated. Once students have "sprouted" (risen to their knees with their arms by their sides), ask students if plants grow quickly or slowly (slowly). Demonstrate to students how to mimic plant growth by slowly lifting one arm and then the other, and then gradually standing up. Next, with students still on their knees with their arms at their sides, darken the room and then ask students if plants will grow in the dark. As students to name things that a young plant needs to grow (food, water, and light). Tell students that you are now going to provide light and more water, and tell them to act out how plants grow like you did, reminding them that plants grow slowly. Shine the flashlight on students, then spray water over them. Next, turn on the overhead classroom lights, saying, "look, your plants are in the bright sun now!" and show students how to stand on their tiptoes and reach their arms toward the ceiling lights.

Ask students what they think will happen to plants if they don't get enough light or enough water (they will wilt and will not grow). Demonstrate how a plant wilts by dropping your chin to your chest and lowering your arms to your sides. Next, use the empty spray bottle to attempt to spray water. Point out to students that there is no water coming out and ask students to name what their plants are missing (water) and have them begin to "wilt." Next, turn off the classroom lights and ask students to name what their plants are missing (light) and have them continue "wilting." Then, spritz them with water from the full spray bottle and shine the flashlight on them again, prompting students to remember what they did when their plants' needs were met. Finally, turn the classroom lights back on and have students repeat the motion of standing on their tiptoes and reaching for the ceiling.

STEM Research Notebook Entry #4

Have students document what they learned about how plants grow in their STEM Research Notebooks, using both words and pictures.

Super Sunflowers Investigation

Students will investigate plant growth through the Super Sunflowers investigation. This will be an ongoing investigation throughout the module since students will plant seeds and observe their growth under various conditions. This investigation is designed to simulate drought conditions that might occur if there is little rainfall, and interrupted sunlight from particulate matter in the air (air pollution). Students will plant seeds and watch them grow under three different sets of conditions:

- Investigation #1: seed will be properly watered and have daily access to sunlight

- Investigation #2: seed will be properly watered but will not have access to sunlight

- Investigation #3: seed will not be watered but will have access to sunlight

Students will use the predict/observe/explain process as they investigate the sunflowers' growth and will create STEM Research Notebook entries for each phase of the investigation.

Introduce students to the Super Sunflowers investigation by telling them that they are going to plant seeds and watch them grow in three different sets of conditions that are like conditions in the environment. First, however, tell students that all living things need certain things to survive. Hold a class discussion about the basic needs of living things by asking the following questions:

- What are the basic needs of all living things? (air, water, food, shelter, and sunlight)

- What happens when all five basic needs are not met?

- What are some reasons these basic needs may not be met?

Next, introduce students to each of the three growing conditions for their sunflower seeds (see above) and ask students to predict what will happen to the seeds in each of the conditions, asking:

- What does your seed need to sprout into a seedling?

- How long will it take for your seed to sprout into a seedling?

- How much will your seedling grow each week?

Students will create a STEM Research Notebook entry recording their ideas, and you should also record student ideas on a Predict/Observe/Explain (P.O.E.) chart, a 4-column chart with a column for growing condition, and then one column each for Predict, Observe, and Explain, and a separate row for each of the 3 growing conditions.

STEM Research Notebook Entry #5

Students will record their predictions for the following questions, for each of the three growing conditions:

- What does your seed need to sprout into a seedling?

- How long will it take for your seed to sprout into a seedling?

- How much will your seeding grow each week?

After students have made predictions for each of the three growing conditions, group student in teams of 2 and provide them with the supplies for the Super Sunflowers investigation (the bottom half of 3 clear 2-liter bottles that have been cut in half, potting soil, sunflower seeds, plastic plates).

Direct students in the following procedure for each of the three bottles:

- Fill the bottle bottom with potting soil

- Plant 2 or 3 sunflower seeds in the soil, about 2 inches deep

- Label each bottle with students' names with masking tape and permanent marker

- Each team should cut out one set of the bottle labels included with STEM Research Notebook Entry #5

- Label the bottles by taping one of the 3 labels onto each bottle

- Place each of the bottles on a plastic plate

- Have students fill the plastic cups with about 12 ounces of water and use about half the water to water the seeds in bottle #1 and half the water to water the seeds in bottle #2

- Have students deliver each of the bottles, on its plastic plate, to the areas you have reserved for the investigation.

Students should care for their plants on an ongoing basis and will make their observations over time. Tell students that the seeds should be cared for as follows:

- For bottle #1, water these plants daily (about ¼ cup water) and keep them on the window sill where they will receive daily sunlight (keep the plastic plates under the bottles to contain water leakage).

- For bottle #2, properly water these plants daily (about ¼ cup water) but keep them in a dark area of the classroom to restrict sunlight (keep the plastic plates under the bottles to contain water leakage).

- For bottle #3, do not water these plants but keep them on the window sill where they will receive daily sunlight.

Students' observations will take place over time. You may wish to have students take pictures of their seeds or video record them daily. After about a week (germination typically takes between about three and eight days), have students measure their seedlings using rulers and record their observations in STEM Research Notebook entry #6 and add to the class P.O.E. chart. Have students observe and measure their seedlings two more times at intervals of 4–5 days throughout the module and add their observations to STEM Research Notebook entry #6.

STEM Research Notebook Entry #6

Students will record their Super Sunflowers observations in their STEM Research Notebooks, using both words and pictures.

Hold a class discussion after each observation, asking the following for each of the bottles:

- How long did it take for your seed to sprout into a seedling?

- How much did your seedling grow?

- Which seedling is tallest?

- Which seedling is shortest?

Mathematics and Social Studies Connections: The class should also continue to sort, count, chart, and graph (e.g., number of items, types of items) and compare daily tallies of recyclables each day.

Explanation

ELA and Science Classes: After students have made their Super Sunflowers observations (this will likely be around Week 3 or 4 of the module), remind students of the five basic needs of all living things. As a class, discuss whether each of the growing conditions in the Super Sunflowers investigation provided the plants' basic needs. Have students record their explanations for how these growing conditions influenced the seeds' growth in their STEM Research Notebooks and add to the class P.O.E. chart. Revisit the predictions they made before the investigation and have students compare their predictions to their observations. Discuss whether their predictions were accurate, close, or not accurate, and why.

STEM Research Notebook Entry #7

Students will use their understanding of the five basic needs of living creatures to explain why the sunflower seeds did or did not grow (using words and pictures).

Mathematics Connection: After the sunflower seeds have sprouted, have students measure the height of each of their three sunflower plants on multiple days and record the measurements. Once students have collected several measurements, have students share the measurements as a class and look for patterns among the measurements (for example, the sunflower in investigation #1 may have grown the most for each group).

Social Studies Connection: N.A.

Elaboration/Application of Knowledge

ELA and Science Classes and Social Studies Connection: Introduce the idea to students that their sunflowers are experiencing conditions that are like environmental conditions plants might experience in nature. For example, some plants might not receive adequate water or sunlight if buildings are erected nearby that block the plants access to rain and sun. In addition, air pollution can block plants' access to sunlight if there are enough particles in the air. Remind students that they are going to act as environmental explorers in this module. To do this, they will look carefully at their environment to see whether and how humans have impacted it and how this has influenced plant and animal habitats. As a class, have students brainstorm about ways that humans can influence the environment, creating a class list.

Introduce blogs and newsletters and their role in communities. Allow students to explore a local newspaper or newsletter and/or an age-appropriate blog and share ideas about why communicating information in these ways can be helpful to a community.

End of Lesson Assessment: Assess student learning by having students define the term "environment" using words and pictures and using a minimum of two vocabulary words. Pair students and have them compare their pictures. Allow students to identify and discuss the differences in their pictures.

Mathematics Connection: Introduce the idea of graphing to students as a way to represent numbers in a picture-like format. Work as a class to create bar graphs of the recyclables collected (e.g., number of aluminum cans, number of paper items, number of plastic items)

Evaluation/Assessment

Students may be assessed on the following performance tasks and other measures listed.

Performance Tasks

- Super Sunflowers investigation
- End of Lesson Assessment

Other Measures (using assessment rubrics in Appendix B)

- Teacher observations
- STEM Research Notebook entries
- Participation in teams during investigations

INTERNET RESOURCES

STEM Teaching Tools resource on formative assessments

- *http://stemteachingtools.org/pd/sessionc*

Learning and Teaching About the Environment

- *www.epa.gov/students*
- "What's the difference between weather and climate?" page at *www.nasa.gov/mission_pages/noaa-n/climate/climate_weather.html*

Bureau of Labor Statistics' *Occupational Outlook Handbook*

- *www.bls.gov/ooh/home.html*

Interactive read-aloud resources

- *www.readingrockets.org/article/repeated-interactive-read-alouds-preschool-and-kindergarten*

- *www.k5chalkbox.com/interactive-read-aloud.html*
- *www.readwritethink.org/professional-development/strategy-guides/teacher-read-aloud-that-30799.html*

"This Land is Your Land" video

- *www.youtube.com/watch?v=3C4iRf9gOdY*

SAMPLE WEATHER SYMBOLS FOR CLASS WEATHER CHART

STUDENT HANDOUT

WEATHER CHART: TODAY'S FORECAST

Date	Temperature	Amount of Sun		Precipitation		Wind		
		Sunny	Partly Sunny	Cloudy	Rain	Snow	Strong Winds	Light Winds	No Wind

Lesson Plan 2
Let's Explore Our Neighborhood Environment!

In this lesson, students will explore pollution and how it affects the environment with an emphasis on littering and air and water pollution. Students will explore the school neighborhood to collect data about the environment and evidence of human impacts on the environment. Students will explore the potential to repurpose garbage items as they use the engineering design process (EDP) to create toys from waste items.

ESSENTIAL QUESTIONS

- What is pollution?
- How does pollution affect the environment?
- How does pollution affect habitats?
- How does pollution affect the basic needs of all living things?
- How can recycling help to reduce the effects of littering on the environment?

ESTABLISHED GOALS AND OBJECTIVES

At the conclusion of this lesson, students will be able to do the following:

- Identify and describe living (animals, insects, and plants) components of their school neighborhood
- Identify features of their school neighborhood that can be smelled and heard
- Define pollution
- Describe how pollution affects the environment, habitats, and all living things
- Describe several ways that human activity causes pollution
- Describe several ways that people can prevent pollution or clean up the effects of pollution
- Understand local weather patterns and be able to make connections between the weather and local environmental conditions
- Understand the influence of recycling of materials used in consumer products on the environment
- Describe the EDP as the process engineers use to solve problems
- Use the EDP to turn waste items into toys
- Identify technological advances and tools that scientists use to learn about changes in the environment

TIME REQUIRED

12 days (approximately 30 minutes each day; see Tables 3.7–3.9, pp. 38–39)

MATERIALS

Required Materials for Lesson 2

- STEM Research Notebooks

- Computer with internet access for viewing videos

- iPads, smartphones, or tablets for student videotaping (optional)

- EDP graphic (optional handout per student; attached at the end of this lesson on p. 86)

- Books

    o *Water Pollution* by Rhonda Lucas Donald

    o *Air Pollution* by Rhonda Lucas Donald

    o *One Plastic Bag: Isatou Ceesay and the Recycling Women of Gambia* by Miranda Paul and Elizabeth Zunon

- Chart paper

- Markers

- U.S. Map

- Materials for water filter design and demonstration (1 per class unless otherwise noted)

    o 1 empty plastic water bottle (about 16 ounces) with the bottom cut off about 1 inch from the bottom of the bottle and a small hole in the cap

    o 2 clear 16 ounce plastic cups – 1 empty and 1 filled with "polluted" water

    o 12 ounces of water

    o Materials to create of polluted water (e.g., 2 tablespoons of vegetable oil, 1 tablespoon of dirt, small pieces of colored plastic)

    o 1 coffee filter

    o ¼ cup sand

    o ¼ cup pea gravel

    o 1 piece of white paper per student

- Small fan for air pollution demonstration

- Plastic straws (1 per student)

- Sandwich sized zipper seal plastic bags (1 per student)

Additional Materials for Trash to Toys Design Challenge
Materials to create a sample project (e.g., pizza box, bottle caps, permanent markers – see Lesson Preparation, pp. 75–76)
Design kit (1 per team of 3–4 students):

- 2 scissors

- Masking tape (1 roll)

- 2 glue sticks (1 for each group of 3–4 students)

- 1 ball of string

- 10 pipe cleaners

- 10 rubber bands

Other materials (per team of 3–4 students or a class selection from which student teams can choose) such as:

Egg carton

Milk jug or carton

Cardboard box/cereal box

Can (be sure there are no sharp edges)

Paper towel or toilet paper rolls

sheets of newspaper

Gallon size Ziploc bags of packing peanuts

Fabric scraps

Yogurt containers or other plastic containers

SAFETY NOTES

1. Students should use caution when handling scissors, as the sharp points and blades can cut or puncture skin.

2. Tell students to be careful when handling recycled bottles and cans. Cans may have sharp edges, which can cut or puncture skin. Glass or plastic bottles can break and cut skin.

3. Have students wash hands with soap and water after the activity is completed.

CONTENT STANDARDS AND KEY VOCABULARY

Table 4.4 lists the content standards from the *NGSS, CCSS*, NAEYC, and the Framework for 21st Century Learning that this lesson addresses, and Table 4.5 (p. 73) presents the key vocabulary. Vocabulary terms are provided for both teacher and student use. Teachers may choose to introduce some or all of the terms to students.

Table 4.4. Standards Addressed in STEM Road Map Module Lesson Two

---

NEXT GENERATION SCIENCE STANDARDS
PERFORMANCE EXPECTATIONS

- K-LS1-1. Use observations to describe patterns of what plants and animals (including humans) need to survive.

- K-ESS2-1. Use and share observations of local weather conditions to describe patterns over time.

- K-ESS2-2. Construct an argument supported by evidence for how plants and animals (including humans) can change the environment to meet their needs.

- K-ESS3-1. Use a model to represent the relationship between the needs of different plants and animals (including humans) and the places they live.

- K-PS3-1. Make observations to determine the effect of sunlight on Earth's surface.

SCIENCE AND ENGINEERING PRACTICES
Analyzing and Interpreting Data

- Analyzing data in K-2 builds on prior experiences and progresses to collecting, recording, and sharing observations.

- Use observations (firsthand or from media) to describe patterns in the natural world in order to answer scientific questions.

Developing and Using Models

- Modeling in K-2 builds on prior experiences and progresses to include using and developing models (i.e., diagram, drawing, physical replica, diorama, dramatization, storyboard) that represent concrete events or design solutions.

- Use a model to represent relationships in the natural world.

Continued

Table 4.4. (*continued*)

Planning and Carrying Out Investigations

- Planning and carrying out investigations to answer questions or test solutions to problems in K-2 builds on prior experiences and progresses to simple investigations, based on fair tests, which provide data to support explanations or design solutions.

- Make observations (firsthand or from media) to collect data that can be used to make comparisons.

DISCIPLINARY CORE IDEAS

LS1.C. *Organization for Matter and Energy Flow in Organisms*

- All animals need food in order to live and grow. They obtain their food from plants or from other animals. Plants need water and light to live and grow.

ESS3.A. *Natural Resources*

- Living things need water, air, and resources from the land, and they live in places that have the things they need. Humans use natural resources for everything they do.

PS3.B. *Conservation of Energy and Energy Transfer*

- Sunlight warms Earth's surface.

CROSSCUTTING CONCEPTS

Patterns

- Patterns in the natural and human designed world can be observed and used as evidence.

Systems and System Models

- Systems in the natural and designed world have parts that work together.

Cause and Effect

- Events have causes that generate observable patterns.

COMMON CORE STATE STANDARDS FOR MATHEMATICS

MATHEMATICAL PRACTICES

- MP1. Make sense of problems and persevere in solving them.

- MP2. Reason abstractly and quantitatively.

- MP3. Construct viable arguments and critique the reasoning of others.

- MP4. Model with mathematics.

- MP5. Use appropriate tools strategically.

- MP6. Attend to precision.

- MP7. Look for and make use of structure.

- MP8. Look for and express regularity in repeated reasoning.

MATHEMATICAL CONTENT

- K.CC.B.4. Understand the relationship between numbers and quantities; connect counting to cardinality.

- K.CC.B.4a. When counting objects, say the number names in the standard order, pairing each object with one and only one number name and each number name with one and only one object.

- K.CC.B.4b. Understand that the last number name said tells the number of objects counted. The number of objects is the same regardless of their arrangement or the order in which they were counted.

- K.CC.B.4c. Understand that each successive number name refers to a quantity that is one larger.

- K.CC.C.6. Identify whether the number of objects in one group is greater than, less than, or equal to the number of objects in another group, e.g., by using matching and counting strategies.

- K.CC.C.7. Compare two numbers between 1 and 10 presented as written numerals.

- K.MD.A.1. Describe measurable attributes of objects, such as length or weight. Describe several measurable attributes of a single object.

- K.MD.A.2. Directly compare two objects with a measurable attribute in common, to see which object has "more of"/"less of" the attribute, and describe the difference. For example, directly compare the heights of two children and describe one child as taller/shorter.

- K.MD.B.3. Classify objects into given categories; count the numbers of objects in each category and sort the categories by count.

COMMON CORE STATE STANDARDS FOR ENGLISH LANGUAGE ARTS
READING STANDARDS

- RI.K.1. With prompting and support, ask and answer questions about key details in a text.

- RI.K.3. With prompting and support, describe the connection between two individuals, events, ideas, or pieces of information in a text.

WRITING STANDARDS

- W.K.2 Use a combination of drawing, dictating, and writing to compose informative/explanatory texts in which they name what they are writing about and supply some information about the topic.

Continued

Table 4.4. (*continued*)

- W.K.5 With guidance and support from adults, respond to questions and suggestions from peers and add details to strengthen writing as needed.

- W.K.7 Participate in shared research and writing projects (e.g., explore a number of books by a favorite author and express opinions about them).

SPEAKING AND LISTENING STANDARDS

- SL.K.1. Participate in collaborative conversations with diverse partners about kindergarten topics and texts with peers and adults in small and larger groups.

- SL.K.3. Ask and answer questions in order to seek help, get information, or clarify something that is not understood.

- SL.K.5. Add drawings or other visual displays to descriptions as desired to provide additional detail.

NATIONAL ASSOCIATION FOR THE EDUCATION OF YOUNG CHILDREN STANDARDS

2.G.02. Children are provided varied opportunities and materials to learn key content and principles of science.

2.G.03. Children are provided with varied opportunities and materials that encourage them to use the five senses to observe, explore, and experiment with scientific phenomena.

2.G.04. Children are provided with varied opportunities to use simple tools to observe objects and scientific phenomena.

2.G.05. Children are provided with varied opportunities and materials to collect data and to represent and document their findings (e.g., through drawing or graphing).

2.G.06. Children are provided with varied opportunities and materials that encourage them to think, question, and reason about observed and inferred phenomena.

2.G.07. Children are provided with varied opportunities and materials that encourage them to discuss scientific concepts in everyday conversation.

2.G.08. Children are provided with varied opportunities and materials that help them learn and use scientific terminology and vocabulary associated with the content areas.

2.H.02. All children have opportunities to access technology that they can use.

2.H.03. Technology is used to extend learning within the classroom and integrate and enrich the curriculum.

FRAMEWORK FOR 21ST CENTURY LEARNING

Interdisciplinary Themes; Learning and Innovation Skills; Information, Media and Technology Skills; Life and Career Skills

Table 4.5. Key Vocabulary for Lesson Two

Key Vocabulary	Definition
air	the invisible gases that surround us and provide the oxygen we need to live
engineering	creating or building something to meet a need or solve a problem
filter	to remove dirt or pollutants from a liquid
gas	substance that floats around us and is invisible
oxygen	a gas that humans and other animals need to live
pollutant	the particles or substances that make up pollution
reuse	to use something more than one time

TEACHER BACKGROUND INFORMATION

In this lesson, students will begin to use the engineering design process (EDP) as they design and build toys using waste materials (Trash to Toys Design Challenge activity).

Engineering

Students will begin to gain an understanding of engineering as a profession through using the EDP. In particular, they should understand that engineers are people who design and build products and systems in response to human needs. For an overview of the various types of engineering professions, see the following websites:

- https://www.engineergirl.org

- www.nacme.org/types-of-engineering

- www.sciencekids.co.nz/sciencefacts/engineering/typesofengineeringjobs.html

Engineering Design Process

Students should understand that engineers need to work in groups to accomplish their work, and that collaboration is important for designing solutions to problems. Students will use the engineering design process (EDP), the same process that professional engineers use in their work, in this lesson. A graphic representation of the EDP is provided at the end of this lesson; it may be useful to post this in your classroom. You should be prepared to review each step of the EDP listed on the graphic with students. It may be useful to post this in your classroom. Be prepared to review the steps of the EDP with

students and emphasize that the process is not a linear one - at any point in the process they may need to return to a previous step. You may wish to provide each student with a copy of the EDP graphic and/or post it in a prominent place in the classroom for student reference throughout the module. The steps of the process are:

1. *Define.* Students should specify what the problem is that they are trying to solve and identify any constraints and limitations that they face in creating a solution.

2. *Learn.* Students brainstorm solutions and conduct relevant research during this step.

3. *Plan.* Students should plan their work here, including making sketches and dividing tasks among team members if necessary.

4. *Try.* Students will build a device, create a system, or complete a product during this step.

5. *Test.* During this step, teams should test their solutions. This might be done by a performance test if they have created a device to accomplish a task or by asking for feedback from others about their solution.

6. *Decide.* Based on what students found out during the "try" phase, they can adjust their solution or make changes to their device.

7. *Share.* During this stage, students will share their solution or device with others. This represents an additional opportunity for students to receive feedback and make modifications based upon that feedback.

The following are additional resources about the EDP:

*   *www.sciencebuddies.org/engineering-design-process/engineering-design-compare-scientific-method.shtml*

*   *www.pbslearningmedia.org/resource/phy03.sci.engin.design.desprocess/what-is-the-design-process/*

COMMON MISCONCEPTIONS

Students will have various types of prior knowledge about the concepts introduced in this lesson. Table 4.6 outlines some common misconceptions students may have concerning these concepts. Because of the breadth of students' experiences, it is not possible to anticipate every misconception that students may bring as they approach this lesson. Incorrect or inaccurate prior understanding of concepts can influence student learning in the future, however, so it is important to be alert to misconceptions such as those presented in the table.

Table 4.6. Common Misconceptions About the Concepts in Lesson 2

Topic	Student Misconception	Explanation
Environmental Science	Pollution is always visible.	Pollution can be caused by particles too small to be seen by the unaided human eye. For example, chemicals that contaminate water are not visible, and many types of air pollutants are not visible.
	Pollution is only from man-made (not natural) sources	Natural phenomena such as volcanoes, forest fires, and decaying vegetation emit particles that can pollute the air or water.
	Trees are not plants.	Trees are plants.
Engineers and the engineering design process (EDP)	All engineers are people who drive trains.	Railroad engineers are just one type of engineer. The engineers referred to in this module are people who use science, technology, and mathematics to build machines, products, and structures that meet people's needs.
	Engineers use only science and mathematics to do their work.	Engineers often use science and mathematics in their work, but they also use many other kinds of knowledge to solve problems and design products, such as how people use products, what people's needs are, and how the natural environment affects materials.

PREPARATION FOR LESSON 2

Review the Teacher Background Information (pp. 73–74), assemble the materials for the lesson, duplicate the EDP graphic (p. 86) if you wish to hand it out to students or enlarge it to post in the classroom, and preview the videos recommended in the Learning Components section that follows.

Prepare "polluted" water for the water pollution demonstration by filling a 16 ounce clear plastic cup of water about 2/3 full and adding objects and other filterable materials. Prepare a water bottle to act as the outer container for the filtering mechanism by cutting off the bottom 1 inch of the bottle and creating a small hole in the bottle cap. Replace the bottle cap. The class will be challenged to devise a design for a water filter using the materials provided. The class will create the design for the water filter using the given materials. You may wish to experiment with the materials in advance. Students will likely devise something like the following design: the

upside down water bottle is placed within the plastic cup; the coffee filter is placed inside the water bottle so that it touches the cap, with sand and gravel layered in the coffee filter; the "polluted" water is then poured through the filter and collected in the plastic cup.

Students will take walks through the school neighborhood as they investigate the environmental health of the neighborhood. Plan to take at least two of these walking tours. Check weather each day for the walking tour and make appropriate accommodations (e.g. raincoats, umbrellas, hats, etc.). You may wish to prepare a neighborhood scavenger hunt to guide students' first walking tour. If you choose to do this, prepare by touring the area students will access during the walking tours to identify a variety of habitat features that they may see (for example, a particular kind of tree with distinctive bark or other plants found near the school, a bird's nest, a birdfeeder, a piece of litter on the ground). Take a picture of each item and include each picture on a student handout you create titled "Neighborhood Explorers Scavenger Hunt," with a blank beside each picture that students will check off when they find that item.

You should collect waste materials/recyclables for the Trash to Toys Design Challenge activity. You may choose to use some of the recyclables from the class recycling program, and you may also have students bring an additional assortment of other waste materials (egg cartons, boxes, cans, milk jugs, plastic bottles, packing materials, newspapers, fabric scraps, etc.) from home to create a set of materials for students to work with. You may wish to enlist the assistance of adult volunteers or older students to work with teams as they move through the steps of the EDP for this activity.

You should create a sample toy to show students before they begin the Trash to Toys Design Challenge. Using materials that the students to which the students will not have access during the activity will ensure that students do not copy your design. For example, you may wish to create a simple tic-tac-toe board and game pieces using an empty pizza box, and ten water bottle caps (five each of two different colors).

LEARNING COMPONENTS
Introductory Activity/Engagement

Connection to the Challenge: Begin each day of this lesson by directing students' attention to the module challenge, the Environmental Explorers Challenge:

> *Your class has been challenged to teach other students at your school about the plant and animal habitats in your area, and ways that they can care for the environment to protect these habitats and make sure that your town's environment is clean and healthy for people as well as other animals and plants.*

Remind students of the driving question for the module: How can we care for the environment?

On each day of the lesson, hold a brief class discussion of how students' learning in the previous days' lessons contributed to their ability to complete the challenge. You may wish to create a class list of key ideas on chart paper.

ELA and Science Classes: Introduce the concept of pollution through a class discussion, documenting student responses on a KWL chart. Ask students:

- What is pollution?

- How does pollution happen?

- How does pollution affect the environment?

- How does pollution affect habitats?

- How can pollution affect living things?

Introduce the concept that there are different types of pollution. Ask students to share their ideas about what types of pollution there are. Guide students to understand that air pollution, water pollution, and littering can all affect our environment.

Hold up the jar of polluted water you prepared (see Lesson Preparation, pp. 75–76). Ask students to observe what they see in the water and where these pollutants may have come from. Ask students to share their ideas for whether or not this water would be healthy for animals, like fish, that live in the water and why they think this. Tell students that as a class they will try to find a way to make this water healthier for fish and other animals. Ask students to share their ideas about how they could do this, making a class list of students' ideas.

Next, show students the plastic cup, prepared water bottle, coffee filter, sand, and gravel, and tell students that you have only these materials to use these to clean the water. Group students in teams of 3–4 and distribute a sheet of white paper to each student and display the materials where all students can see them. Instruct students to discuss in their teams their ideas about how the water could be cleaned. After five minutes, ask each student to draw a picture of how they think that these materials could clean the "polluted" water. After students have completed their drawing, have several students share their designs with the class.

After several designs have been displayed, hold a class discussion about which design would work best (e.g., a design in which the filter is placed inside the plastic cup is on the right track, but if there are no holes in the bottom of the cup, the water in the filter will not be able to drain through). As a class, decide on a design for the water filter and created a labeled sketch of the design on chart paper or on a whiteboard. Build the filter according to the class's suggested design and pour water through it.

Ask the class for their ideas about how the filter worked (i.e., is clean water captured in a separate container?) and how it might be improved to work better with the current materials and then how the design might be improved if the class had more materials available.

Next, students will explore water pollution through an interactive read aloud of *Water Pollution* by Rhonda Lucas Donald. Students will complete STEM Research Notebook entries after reading. You should also document student responses on a KWL chart.

STEM Research Notebook Entry #8

Have students document what they learned about water pollution in their STEM Research Notebooks, using both words and pictures.

Mathematics Connection: N.A.

Social Studies Connection: Ask students what changes in the environment they have heard about (for example droughts in California, air pollution in large cities, etc.). As students share their experiences and use the map to identify the places where these changes are occurring. Discuss how these changes influence people, plants, and animals, and hold a class discussion about why those changes might be happening.

Activity/Exploration

ELA Class and Science Classes and Mathematics and Social Studies Connection:
Activities for this lesson include:

- Exploring water pollution through viewing a video

- Exploring the school neighborhood in Our Neighborhood Environmental Health walking tours

- Exploring air pollution through an interactive read aloud

- Exploring litter and recycling through an interactive read aloud (an introduction to the Trash to Toys Design Challenge activity that students complete in the Extension/Application of Knowledge section)

Remind student that there are different types of pollution. Ask students what they know about water pollution and its causes. Students will continue to explore water pollution by viewing a video about water pollution such as "Animated Lesson to learn about Water Pollution" at *www.youtube.com/watch?v=y1ObvXZDQNs*. Students will create STEM Research Notebook entries after watching the video. You should also document student responses on a KWL chart.

4

STEM Research Notebook Entry #9

Have students document what they learned about water pollution and prevention of water pollution in their STEM Research Notebooks, using both words and pictures.

Our Neighborhood Environmental Health Investigation

Prepare for the investigation by holding a class discussion about your geographic location and the habitats, animals, and plants found in your area. Have students work as a class to identify your location on a map. Ask students:

- Where do we live? (Locate on map and globe)

- What is the habitat like where we live (for example, are there forests, mountains, an ocean nearby)?

- What is the climate like where we live?

- What are some types of animals and plants where we live?

As a class, create a chart listing student responses. Have students complete STEM Research Notebook Entry #10 with this information.

STEM Research Notebook Entry #10

Have students record the information about their geographic area from the class discussion, using both words and pictures.

Ask students to predict how many animals they could observe near their school and how many plants they could observe. Record these predictions. Tell students that they will be acting as environmental explorers by using nature as their classroom. Tell students that they will go out into the school neighborhood to observe and collect information about animals, plants, ways people have impacted the environment, and other clues about the environment such as smells and sounds.

As a class, work together to devise a list of guidelines for staying safe as environmental explorers. Ask students to share their ideas, documenting students' ideas on chart paper. Encourage students to include safety guidelines (e.g., stay with a partner or with the class, don't touch plants [some plants, such as poison ivy, may be harmful], don't touch insects or animals, don't litter). Review the class guidelines before embarking on the walking tours.

Have students take at least two walking tours of the school neighborhood for this investigation. Students will create STEM Research Notebook Entry #11 during or after the walking tours. You may wish to allow students to video record or take photographs of their findings with I-pads/phones/tablets, etc.

STEM Research Notebook Entry #11

Have students document their observations of the school neighborhood in their STEM Research Notebooks, using both words and pictures.

When the class returns from the walking tour hold a class discussion about their observations, comparing the numbers of plants and animals they observed with their predictions, asking students whether their predictions were higher or lower than the actual numbers observed. Create a bar graph of student observations from the Our Neighborhood Environmental Health walking tours. For example, you could graph the number of animals, trees and other plants, examples of litter, and human causes of habitat changes (e.g., buildings, roads, sidewalks) students observed.

Next, introduce air pollution with a class discussion about air, asking students the following questions:

- What is air?

- Where is air found?

- Do we need air to live?

- Do animals and plants need air to live?

- Can we see air?

- If we can't see air, how do we know it's there?

Next, turn on a fan and have students put their hands about 12 inches in front of it. Ask them to describe what they feel. Tell students that what they are feeling is air moving. Ask students if they have ever smelled food cooking in another room, or perfume that someone is wearing. Explain to students that they are smelling gases from the cooking food or from the perfume that move with the moving air. Ask students again, "if we can't see air, how do we know it's there?" prompting students to understand that we can experience the effects of air moving. Ask students to name some examples of times when they experience the effects of air moving (e.g., wind blows their hair, smelling food cooking or other odors like a skunk's spray, breathing in and out, blowing up a balloon). Give each student a plastic straw and a zipper seal bag. Demonstrate to students how to insert the end of the straw into the bag and close the zipper seal around the straw. Next ask students to blow gently into their straws and observe what happens. Ask students what they think will happen if they blow harder, then let students experiment with blowing into the straws gently and harder. As a class, discuss what students observed. Tell students that they are observing air moving.

Have students explore air pollution through an interactive read aloud of *Air Pollution* by Rhonda Lucas Donald. Students will create STEM Research Notebook entries after the reading. You should also document student responses on a KWL chart.

STEM Research Notebook Entry #12

Students will document what they learned about air pollution in their STEM Research Notebooks, using both words and pictures.

As a class, discuss whether students saw any evidence of air pollution on their neighborhood walk (e.g., smells) and why air pollution might be difficult to see.

Trash to Toys Design Challenge Introduction

Next, introduce the Trash to Toys Design Challenge activity by introducing the term *litter,* and holding a class discussion about the effects of litter on the environment and what people can do about it. Document students' litter solutions on chart paper. Introduce the idea that people can sometimes use litter in creative ways. Conduct an interactive read aloud of *One Plastic Bag: Isatou Ceesay and the Recycling Women of Gambia* by Miranda Paul and Elizabeth Zunon. There is no STEM Research Notebook entry associated with this reading since it serves as an introduction to the Trash to Toys Design Challenge activity. Ask students to share their observations of what the characters in the story did to influence the environment.

Explanation

ELA and Science Classes and Social Studies Connection: Add to the vocabulary chart with vocabulary from the interactive read alouds and have students add vocabulary terms to their STEM Research Notebooks, using STEM Research Notebook template #2.

Remind students that they are going to create a newsletter or blog to inform other students about their neighborhood and its environmental health. Have students brainstorm ideas about what information they could use from their Our Neighborhood Environmental Health walking tours to include in their newsletter or blog. If students took photographs during their walking tours, have them identify photos that they could include in their newsletter or blog. Alternatively, have students draw pictures of things they want to include in their newsletter or blog.

Introduce students to the EDP by connecting the idea of design to the book *One Plastic Bag: Isatou Ceesay and the Recycling Women of Gambia.* Explain to students that people who design and create things to meet human needs and solve problems are called engineers. Tell students that engineers often work in teams as they design and build things and they use the EDP to help them in their work. Show students the EDP graphic attached to the end of this lesson. Explain to students that they are going to be challenged to act as engineers to find creative solutions for trash like the women in the book did. Remind students of the water filter the class designed together and tell them that they actually used the EDP to design that. Review each step of the EDP and ask students to recall what they did in the class water filter design for that step.

Ask students to share ideas about what they could do with trash other than throw it away or send it to a recycling center. Document student ideas on a chart. Next, show students the tic-tac-toe board or other toy you created (see Lesson Preparation). Tell students that you created this out of materials that might otherwise go to a landfill. Have students identify what materials you used (e.g., pizza box, bottle caps). Tell students that they are going to create toys from trash and will use the EDP as they act as toy engineers in the Trash to Toys Design Challenge activity (see Elaboration/ Application of Knowledge section, pp. 82–84).

Mathematics Connection: Review the class bar charts about students' observations from their Our Neighborhood Environmental Health walking tours. Ask students to share their ideas about whether they could be useful to include in their newsletter or blog and why.

Elaboration/Application of Knowledge

ELA and Science Classes: Students will explore ways to repurpose trash and recyclables by using the EDP to create toys from trash items and recyclables in the Trash to Toys Design Challenge.

Trash to Toys Design Challenge

Remind students that their challenge is to find uses for trash items so that they don't end up as litter. In this activity, they will act as toy engineers, designing and creating toys using trash/recyclables and a simple set of additional materials. Tell students that their goal is to reduce litter and to create a fun, safe, entertaining toy that kindergartners would like to play with. Ask students to think about toys they have at home or toys in the classroom, asking if any of these items could be made with recycled materials (for example, toy cars could be made of recycled plastic and the stuffing inside stuffed animals could be made of shredded fabric from old clothes). The class will work through the steps of the EDP together. You should track each step of the EDP on chart paper. Group students in teams of 3–4 for the activity.

First, show students the supplies they will have to work with (each team will have a set of design kit items and then will be able to choose from the other materials list).

Remind students that engineers use the steps of the EDP to design and build things and that they will use the EDP also. Track student responses and progress for each step of the EDP on chart paper:

Define: Ask students what problem they have been asked to solve.

Learn:

- Ask students what they need to know to do this (what materials they have available, how much time they have).

- Ask students to work in their teams to brainstorm some ideas of toys they could create.

Plan:

- Have each student draw a picture or pictures of the toys they might create. Remind students that they will have to build their toys from the available materials; students' drawings should reflect this.

- Have each team review the pictures the team members drew and decide on one toy they want to create.

- Have team members decide what materials they will need to build this toy.

Try:

- Give students their design kit items

- Allow each team to choose items from the supply of trash/recyclables. Limit teams to one of each item so that all teams have access to items (you may wish to allow students to choose more items once all teams have had a chance to take items).

- Build the toys. Remind students to use their drawings as a reference.

Test:

- Once teams have completed their toys, tell them to try them out.

Decide:

- Ask students if the toys performed as they expected them to.

- Ask students if the toys are fun to play with.

- Ask students if there is anything they could do to improve their toys.

- Allow students to make modifications to their toys based on their tests. You may wish to allow students to choose additional materials.

Share:

- Have student teams decide on a name for their toys.

- Have each team present their toy, giving its name, describing the toy, and demonstrating how it works.

End of Lesson Assessment: Assess student learning by having students define pollution (using words and pictures) and providing three examples of pollution. Students should use a minimum of three vocabulary words.

Mathematics Connection: N.A.

Social Studies Connection: Connect students' observations of their local environment with scientific careers, introducing the idea that scientists regularly observe and measure things that occur in the environment. Identify tools that scientists use to understand changes in the environment (e.g., thermometers, rain gauges, satellite images).

Evaluation/Assessment

Students may be assessed on the following performance tasks and other measures listed.

Performance Tasks

- Our Neighborhood Environmental Health walking tours

- Trash to Toys Design Challenge toys and presentations

- End of Lesson Assessment

Other Measures (see assessment rubric in Appendix B)

- Teacher observations

- STEM Research Notebook entries

- Participation in their teams during investigations

INTERNET RESOURCES

Information about engineering careers

- *https://www.engineergirl.org*

- *www.nacme.org/types-of-engineering*

- *www.sciencekids.co.nz/sciencefacts/engineering/typesofengineeringjobs.html*

EDP resources

- *www.sciencebuddies.org/engineering-design-process/engineering-design-compare-scientific-method.shtml*

- *www.pbskids.org/designsquad/parentseducators/workshop/process.html*

"Animated Lesson to learn about Water Pollution" video

- *www.youtube.com/watch?v=y1ObvXZDQNs*

Figure 4.1. Engineering Design Process

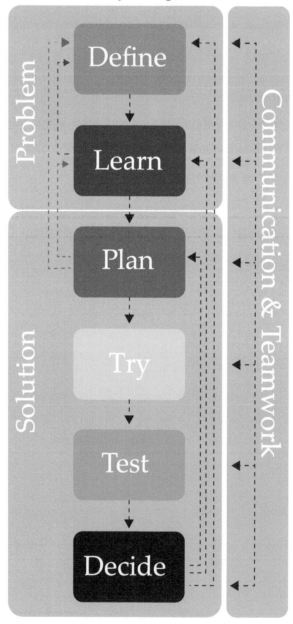

Lesson Plan 3
Neighborhood News

In this lesson, students investigate ways that they can care for the environment. Students will also address the final module challenge in this lesson and will create a school newsletter or blog about the environment in the school neighborhood to be distributed to other kindergarten classes.

ESSENTIAL QUESTIONS

- How can we care for the environment in our school neighborhood?

- How can we share information about the environment in our school neighborhood with other kindergarten students?

- How can we make an action plan for improvements in the environment in our school neighborhood?

ESTABLISHED GOALS AND OBJECTIVES

At the conclusion of this lesson, students will be able to do the following:

- Create and implement a plan to positively impact the local environment

- Understand local weather patterns and be able to make connections between the weather and local environmental conditions

- Describe the local environment using text and illustrations

- Communicate to others via text and illustrations the impacts humans can have on the environment

- Communicate to others via text and illustrations ways that humans can care for the environment

- Produce a class newsletter or blog to report findings about the local environment

TIME REQUIRED

8 days (approximately 30 minutes each day; see Tables 3.9 and 3.10, p. 39)

MATERIALS

Required Materials for Lesson 3

- STEM Research Notebooks

- Computer with internet access for viewing videos

- iPads, smartphones, or tablets for student videotaping (optional)
- Books
  o *Cleaning up Litter* by Charlotte Guillan or *Look Out for Litter* by Lisa Bullard.
- Chart paper
- Markers
- U.S. map
- Local newspaper story related to the environment or clip from local news television show related to the environment

Additional Materials for Good Neighborhood project (project to be decided upon by class). For example:

Tree sapling(s) to plant

Shovel

Gloves for litter cleanup

Trash bags

SAFETY NOTES

1. Students should use caution when handling scissors, as the sharp points and blades can cut or puncture skin.

2. Immediately wipe up any spilled water or soil on the floor to avoid a slip-and-fall hazard.

3. Tell students to be careful when handling recycled bottles and cans. Cans may have sharp edges, which can cut or puncture skin. Glass or plastic bottles can break and cut skin.

4. Have students wash hands with soap and water after the activity is completed.

CONTENT STANDARDS AND KEY VOCABULARY

Table 4.7 lists the content standards from the *NGSS*, *CCSS*, NAEYC, and the Framework for 21st Century Learning that this lesson addresses, and Table 4.8 (p. 92) presents the key vocabulary. Vocabulary terms are provided for both teacher and student use. Teachers may choose to introduce some or all of the terms to students.

Table 4.7. Content Standards Addressed in STEM Road Map Module
Lesson 3

NEXT GENERATION SCIENCE STANDARDS
PERFORMANCE EXPECTATIONS

- K-LS1-1. Use observations to describe patterns of what plants and animals (including humans) need to survive.

- K-ESS2-1. Use and share observations of local weather conditions to describe patterns over time.

- K-ESS2-2. Construct an argument supported by evidence for how plants and animals (including humans) can change the environment to meet their needs.

- K-ESS3-1. Use a model to represent the relationship between the needs of different plants and animals (including humans) and the places they live.

- K-PS3-1. Make observations to determine the effect of sunlight on Earth's surface.

SCIENCE AND ENGINEERING PRACTICES
Analyzing and Interpreting Data

- Analyzing data in K-2 builds on prior experiences and progresses to collecting, recording, and sharing observations.

- Use observations (firsthand or from media) to describe patterns in the natural world in order to answer scientific questions.

Developing and Using Models

- Modeling in K-2 builds on prior experiences and progresses to include using and developing models (i.e., diagram, drawing, physical replica, diorama, dramatization, storyboard) that represent concrete events or design solutions.

- Use a model to represent relationships in the natural world.

Planning and Carrying Out Investigations

- Planning and carrying out investigations to answer questions or test solutions to problems in K-2 builds on prior experiences and progresses to simple investigations, based on fair tests, which provide data to support explanations or design solutions.

- Make observations (firsthand or from media) to collect data that can be used to make comparisons.

DISCIPLINARY CORE IDEAS
LS1.C. *Organization for Matter and Energy Flow in Organisms*

- All animals need food in order to live and grow. They obtain their food from plants or from other animals. Plants need water and light to live and grow.

Continued

Table 4.7. *(continued)*

ESS3.A. *Natural Resources*

• Living things need water, air, and resources from the land, and they live in places that have the things they need. Humans use natural resources for everything they do.

PS3.B. *Conservation of Energy and Energy Transfer*

• Sunlight warms Earth's surface.

CROSSCUTTING CONCEPTS

Patterns

• Patterns in the natural and human designed world can be observed and used as evidence.

Systems and System Models

• Systems in the natural and designed world have parts that work together.

Cause and Effect

• Events have causes that generate observable patterns.

COMMON CORE STATE STANDARDS FOR MATHEMATICS

MATHEMATICAL PRACTICES

• MP1. Make sense of problems and persevere in solving them.

• MP2. Reason abstractly and quantitatively.

• MP3. Construct viable arguments and critique the reasoning of others.

• MP4. Model with mathematics.

• MP5. Use appropriate tools strategically.

• MP6. Attend to precision.

• MP7. Look for and make use of structure.

• MP8. Look for and express regularity in repeated reasoning.

MATHEMATICAL CONTENT

• K.CC.B.4. Understand the relationship between numbers and quantities; connect counting to cardinality.

• K.CC.B.4a. When counting objects, say the number names in the standard order, pairing each object with one and only one number name and each number name with one and only one object.

• K.CC.B.4b. Understand that the last number name said tells the number of objects counted. The number of objects is the same regardless of their arrangement or the order in which they were counted.

- K.CC.B.4c. Understand that each successive number name refers to a quantity that is one larger.

- K.CC.C.6. Identify whether the number of objects in one group is greater than, less than, or equal to the number of objects in another group, e.g., by using matching and counting strategies.

- K.CC.C.7. Compare two numbers between 1 and 10 presented as written numerals.

- K.MD.A.1. Describe measurable attributes of objects, such as length or weight. Describe several measurable attributes of a single object.

- K.MD.A.2. Directly compare two objects with a measurable attribute in common, to see which object has "more of"/"less of" the attribute, and describe the difference. For example, directly compare the heights of two children and describe one child as taller/shorter.

- K.MD.B.3. Classify objects into given categories; count the numbers of objects in each category and sort the categories by count.

COMMON CORE STATE STANDARDS FOR ENGLISH LANGUAGE ARTS
READING STANDARDS

- RI.K.1. With prompting and support, ask and answer questions about key details in a text.

- RI.K.3. With prompting and support, describe the connection between two individuals, events, ideas, or pieces of information in a text.

WRITING STANDARDS

- W.K.2 Use a combination of drawing, dictating, and writing to compose informative/explanatory texts in which they name what they are writing about and supply some information about the topic.

- W.K.5 With guidance and support from adults, respond to questions and suggestions from peers and add details to strengthen writing as needed.

- W.K.7 Participate in shared research and writing projects (e.g., explore a number of books by a favorite author and express opinions about them).

SPEAKING AND LISTENING STANDARDS

- SL.K.1. Participate in collaborative conversations with diverse partners about kindergarten topics and texts with peers and adults in small and larger groups.

- SL.K.3. Ask and answer questions in order to seek help, get information, or clarify something that is not understood.

- SL.K.5. Add drawings or other visual displays to descriptions as desired to provide additional detail.

Continued

Table 4.7. (*continued*)

NATIONAL ASSOCIATION FOR THE EDUCATION OF YOUNG CHILDREN STANDARDS
2.G.02. Children are provided varied opportunities and materials to learn key content and principles of science.
2.G.03. Children are provided with varied opportunities and materials that encourage them to use the five senses to observe, explore, and experiment with scientific phenomena.
2.G.04. Children are provided with varied opportunities to use simple tools to observe objects and scientific phenomena.
2.G.05. Children are provided with varied opportunities and materials to collect data and to represent and document their findings (e.g., through drawing or graphing).
2.G.06. Children are provided with varied opportunities and materials that encourage them to think, question, and reason about observed and inferred phenomena.
2.G.07. Children are provided with varied opportunities and materials that encourage them to discuss scientific concepts in everyday conversation.
2.G.08. Children are provided with varied opportunities and materials that help them learn and use scientific terminology and vocabulary associated with the content areas.
2.H.02. All children have opportunities to access technology that they can use.
2.H.03. Technology is used to extend learning within the classroom and integrate and enrich the curriculum.
FRAMEWORK FOR 21ST CENTURY LEARNING Interdisciplinary Themes; Learning and Innovation Skills; Information, Media and Technology Skills; Life and Career Skills

Table 4.8. Key Vocabulary for Lesson 3

Key Vocabulary	Definition
blog	a web-based publishing platform
statistics	a collection of numbers that describes something

TEACHER BACKGROUND INFORMATION
Blogging with Kindergarten Students

Blogging, or web logging, is a method of web-based publishing that is being used with increasing frequency because of its accessibility and the ease of distributing posts to large numbers of readers. If you choose to use a blog format for the final module challenge, be sure to review your school's safety policies for Internet use and Internet publishing and check with your school administrators for a list of school-approved student blogging sites. You should also request parent permission for students' participation in the blog. An article about blogging with students is available on the Education World website at *www.educationworld.com/a_tech/tech/tech217.shtml*. A template, My Environment News, is provided in Appendix B to guide students in organizing information for their final module challenge.

COMMON MISCONCEPTIONS

Students will have various types of prior knowledge about the concepts introduced in this lesson. Table 4.9 outlines some common misconceptions students may have concerning these concepts. Because of the breadth of students' experiences, it is not possible to anticipate every misconception that students may bring as they approach this lesson. Incorrect or inaccurate prior understanding of concepts can influence student learning in the future, however, so it is important to be alert to misconceptions such as those presented in the table.

Table 4.9. Common Misconceptions About the Concepts in Lesson 3

Topic	Student Misconception	Explanation
Environmental Science	There is nothing people can do to protect habitats.	Humans can protect natural habitats in many ways, including preserving green spaces, planting trees, and reducing pollution.

PREPARATION FOR LESSON 3

Review the Teacher Background Information provided, assemble the materials for the lesson, and preview the videos recommended in the Learning Components section below.

Students will plan and implement a project to care for the neighborhood environment in this lesson (see the Good Neighbors activity in Activity/Exploration section, p. 96). The class will work together to decide on a project to positively impact the environment in the school neighbored (e.g., a neighborhood litter cleanup project or a tree planting project). You will need to make appropriate preparations for these activities, including checking the weather and making sure that students are prepared for weather conditions with appropriate outerwear.

A template for My Environment News, is provided at the end of Appendix A and is intended to help students organize their work for the module challenge. Students will identify the types of information they wish to include in the newsletter or blog in this lesson (see Introductory Activity/Engagement section, pp. 94–95), so you may need to modify the template accordingly (for example, students may choose to include poetry they write about the environment, pictures of them taking their neighborhood walking tour, or information about a neighborhood park). Students should refer to the STEM Research Notebook entries they completed for the Our Neighborhood Environmental Health investigation in Lesson 2 and should incorporate information from their Good Neighbors project and weather chart in their template entries. Have on hand examples of newsletters or blogs created by kindergarteners for students to review.

An option for this lesson is to invite a representative from a local nature center or environmental group to visit the class to talk about a locally relevant environmental issue and how community members can become involved (see the social studies connection in the Elaboration/Application of Knowledge section, pp. 97–98). Make appropriate preparations if you choose to invite a guest speaker, including briefing the guest in advance on developmentally appropriate content for kindergarten students.

LEARNING COMPONENTS

Introductory Activity/Engagement

Connection to the Challenge: Begin each day of this lesson by directing students' attention to the module challenge, the Environmental Explorers Challenge:

> *Your class has been challenged to teach other students at your school about the plant and animal habitats in your area, and ways that they can care for the environment to protect these habitats and make sure that your town's environment is clean and healthy for people as well as other animals and plants.*

Remind students of the driving question for the module: How can we care for the environment?

Tell students that in this lesson they will create a web log or newsletter for other students at their school using what they have learned about habitats in your area, what plants need to grow, pollution, and how people can care for the environment. On each day of the lesson, hold a brief class discussion of how students' learning in the previous days' lessons contributed to their ability to complete the challenge.

ELA and Science Classes: Students will do the following in this lesson:

- Make a class plan to do things to care for the neighborhood environment (see Good Neighbors activity in Activity/Exploration section)

- Implement their Good Neighbors plan and take pictures

- Use their learning from the module to complete the My Environment News template

- Decide as a class what sections and information they will include in the class newsletter or blog

- Decide who will provide information for the sections of the newsletter or blog

- Decide who to distribute the newsletter or blog to

- Create the newsletter or blog

Tell students that one way of caring for the environment is to inform people about what is happening in their neighborhood environment and suggesting ways that they can help to improve the environment. Tell students that they will be caring for the environment in this lesson by a neighborhood project they decide on and by distributing a newsletter or blog.

Show students examples of newsletters or blogs created by kindergarteners. Ask students to share what they like about these newsletters or blogs and what they don't like. Use this information to target the sections and information that the class will include in the newsletter (e.g., including lots of pictures, including personal stories, including information about animals).

If you chose to create a class blog rather than a newsletter, hold a discussion about blogs and blogging. Ask students to share their ideas about the definition of "blog" and why people publish blogs. Introduce students to the blogging site.

Have students explore their potential impact in their world by viewing the video "Change the World In 5 Minutes - Everyday at School" at *www.youtube.com/watch?v=oROsbaxWH0M*. Students will create STEM Research Notebook entries after viewing the video. You should also document student responses on a KWL chart.

STEM Research Notebook Entry #13

Have students document what they learned about how they can make changes in their world in their STEM Research Notebooks, using both words and pictures.

Mathematics Connection: N.A.

Social Studies Connection: Students will use their learning from the "Change the World in 5 Minutes – Everyday at School" video as inspiration to plan and implement their own project to improve the neighborhood environment. Students might choose, for example, to pick up litter, place a recycling unit near the school, or plant a tree. Hold a class discussion about citizenship and caring for the environment, using the students' ideas about the video to draw connections between these concepts.

Activity/Exploration

ELA Class and Science Classes and Social Studies Connection: The class will formulate and carry out a plan for improving the local environment.

Good Neighbors Activity

Introduce the Good Neighbors activity by having the class brainstorm ideas about things they can do to care for the neighborhood environment. Create a class list of ideas. Students will explore two ways they can care for the environment, collecting litter and planting trees.

Students will consider a litter cleanup project through an interactive read aloud of either *Cleaning up Litter* by Charlotte Guillan or *Look Out for Litter* by Lisa Bullard. Students will create STEM Research Notebook after reading. You should also document student responses on a KWL chart.

STEM Research Notebook Entry #14

Have students document what they learned about litter and cleaning up litter in their STEM Research Notebooks, using both words and pictures.

Next, hold a class discussion about how planting trees can be a way to care for the environment. Have students share ideas about how trees can be good for the environment, then conduct an interactive read-aloud of the "Plant a Tree" page on the United States Geological Survey website at *www.usgs.gov/educational-resources/plant-tree*. Students will create STEM Research Notebook entries after the read aloud. You should also document student responses on a KWL chart.

STEM Research Notebook Entry #15

Have students document what they learned about planting trees in their STEM Research Notebooks after the read aloud, using both words and pictures.

Have students decide on a class project to care for the environment from the list they created. The class should implement this plan during the remaining days of the module. Students should take pictures or videos of the project to include in their newsletter or blog.

Students should use their Our Neighborhood Environmental Health STEM Research Notebook entries as well as their class Good Neighbors project and their other learning throughout the module to complete the My Environment News template in preparation for creating their final class newsletter or blog.

Mathematics Connection: N.A.

Social Studies Connection: Continue the discussion of citizenship you began in the Introductory/Engagement portion of this lesson. Discuss the importance of being an informed citizen. Ask students to share ideas about how they can stay informed about what happens in their communities (e.g., reading the newspaper, watching the local television news, accessing news on the Internet, attending community meetings).

As a class, read or watch a local news article or story that is related to environmental health. Have students share their ideas about the environmental issue featured in the story and how people in the community might become involved.

Explanation

ELA and Science Classes and Social Studies Connection: Students should make decisions about their newsletter or blog. Hold a class discussion to make decisions about the following (recording class decisions on chart paper):

- A name for the newsletter or blog

- What sections and information they will include in the class newsletter or blog

- Who will provide information for the sections of the newsletter or blog

- Who to distribute the newsletter or blog to (remind students that the target audience is other kindergarteners; students may also wish to share it with parents/families, preschool classes, and school administrators)

Mathematics Connections: As a class, work to estimate how many readers your newsletter or blog will have based upon each of the audiences the class decided upon. Record an estimate for each group (e.g., other kindergartners, other kindergarten teachers, parents, administrators) and create a bar chart to show the audience distribution for the publication. If the class will be producing a paper newsletter, use the class estimate to decide how many copies of the newsletter they will need.

Elaboration/Application of Knowledge

ELA and Science Classes and Social Studies Connection: Have students create, assemble, and distribute their newsletter or blog.

As a class, review the newsletter or blog and ask students to identify additional things they could do to improve the school neighborhood's environment (e.g., put up a birdfeeder, create a butterfly garden). Create a class list of students' ideas.

An option for this lesson is to have students create an action plan to improve the school environment (note that this will be a project that will be completed after the conclusion of this module and may be an ongoing project). If you choose to do this, tell students that they will create a plan to improve the school environment. From the list students created, have students choose an item that they are interested in taking action on. As a class, discuss what they will need to do to take this action (e.g., get permission from the school principal, make plans to pay for items). Create a class action plan on a piece of chart paper by working as a class to answer the following questions:

- What action will we take?

- How will this make our school neighborhood a better place to live for people, animals, and plants?

- Who do we need to get permission from to do this?

- How will we ask for permission?

- If this action will cost money, how will we pay for it?

- What materials or supplies do we need to do this?

- When will we take this action?

- If our action requires us to take care of something, how will we do this (for example, will we need to fill a birdfeeder or water plants)?

- How will we keep track of our progress (for example, measure plants, count birds at the birdfeeder during certain times of the day and make a graph)?

End of Lesson Assessment: To assess student learning, have students draw and label three ways that they can care for the local environment, using a minimum of three vocabulary words.

Mathematics Connections: Ask the class to share their ideas about how they could find out how many people read their blog, recording student ideas on a class list. After students have distributed their newsletter or blog, determine how many individuals received it (either by number of paper newsletter copies distributed or how many readers accessed the blog if blog statistics are available). Compare this total to the total number of readers the class estimated. Discuss why these numbers may be different.

Optional Social Studies Connection: Invite a local nature center representative, representative from an environmental organization, beekeeper, master gardener, or water quality scientist to speak to the class about a locally relevant environmental issue and ways that community members can be involved.

Evaluation/Assessment

Students may be assessed on the following performance tasks and other measures listed.

Performance Tasks

- Good Neighbors class project

- Class newsletter or blog

- End of Lesson Assessment

Other Measures (see assessment rubric in Appendix B)

- Teacher observations

- STEM Research Notebook entries

- Participation in their teams during investigations

INTERNET RESOURCES

Blogging with students

- *www.educationworld.com/a_tech/tech/tech217.shtml*

"Change The World In 5 Minutes - Everyday at School" video

- *www.youtube.com/watch?v=oROsbaxWH0M*

United States Geological Survey tree planting instructions

- *www.usgs.gov/educational-resources/plant-tree*

SUGGESTED BOOKS

Bergen, L. 2009. *Don't Throw That Away!: A Lift-the-Flap Book about Recycling and Reusing*. New York: Little Simon.

Berger, M. 1994. *Oil Spill*. New York: Harper Collins.

Bullard, L. 2011. *Look Out for Litter*. Millbrook Press.

Cherry, L., and Braasch, G. 2008. *How we know what we know about our changing climate: Scientists and kids explore global warming*. Nevada City, CA: Dawn Publications.

Cherry, L. 1992. *A river ran wild: an environmental history*. San Diego, CA: Harcourt Brace Jovanovich

Cherry, L. 1990. *The Great Kapok Tree: A Tale of the Amazon Rain Forest*. New York: Scholastic.

Donald, R. 2001. *Air Pollution*. New York: Children's Press.

Donald, R. 2001. *Water Pollution*. New York: Children's Press.

Ehlert, L. 1991. *Red Leaf, Yellow Leaf*. San Diego, CA: Harcourt Brace & Company.

Guillan, C. 2008. *Cleaning up Litter*. Heineman.

Lawrence, E. 2014. *Global Warming*. New York: Bearport Publishing.

Lishak, A. 2008. *Global Warming: What's that got to do with me?* North Mankato, MN: Smart Apple Media.

Morgan, S. 2007. *Waste Disposal*. North Mankato, MN: Sea-to-Sea Publications.

Paul, M. and Zunon, E. 2015. *One Plastic Bag: Isatou Ceesay and the Recycling Women of Gambia*. Millbrook Picture Books.

Robinson, F. 1995. *Recycle That!* Chicago: Children's Press.

Robinson, F. 1995. *Too Much Trash!* New York: Children's Press.

Rogers, K. and Alexander, J. 2000. *Paper Crunch*. Crystal Lake, IL: Rigby Literacy.

Siddals, M. 2010. *Compost Stew: An A to Z Recipe for the Earth*. New York: Tricycle Press.

Simon, S. 2010. *Global Warming*. New York: HarperCollins.

REFERENCES

Koehler, C., Bloom, M. A., and Milner, A. R. 2015. The STEM road map for grades K-2. In C. C. Johnson, E. E. Peters-Burton, and T. J. Moore (Eds.), *STEM road map: A framework for integrated STEM education* (pp. 41–67). New York, NY: Routledge. *www.routledge.com/products/9781138804234*.

TRANSFORMING LEARNING WITH OUR CHANGING ENVIRONMENT AND THE *STEM ROAD MAP CURRICULUM SERIES*

Carla C. Johnson

This chapter serves as a conclusion to the Our Changing Environment integrated STEM curriculum module, but it is just the beginning of the transformation of your classroom that is possible through use of the *STEM Road Map Curriculum Series*. In this book, many key resources have been provided to make learning meaningful for your students through integration of science, technology, engineering, and mathematics, as well as social studies and English language arts, into powerful problem- and project-based instruction. First, the Our Changing Environment curriculum is grounded in the latest theory of learning for students in kindergarten specifically. Second, as your students work through this module, they engage in using the engineering design process (EDP) and build prototypes like engineers and STEM professionals in the real world. Third, students acquire important knowledge and skills grounded in national academic standards in mathematics, English language arts, science, and 21st century skills that will enable their learning to be deeper, retained longer, and applied throughout, illustrating the critical connections within and across disciplines. Finally, authentic formative assessments, including strategies for differentiation and addressing misconceptions, are embedded within the curriculum activities.

The Our Changing Environment curriculum in the Optimizing the Human Condition STEM Road Map theme can be used in single-content classrooms (e.g., mathematics) where there is only one teacher or expanded to include multiple teachers and content areas across classrooms. Through the exploration of the Environmental Explorers Challenge, students engage in a real-world STEM problem on the first day

DOI: 10.4324/9781003261728-7

of instruction and gather necessary knowledge and skills along the way in the context of solving the problem.

The other topics in the *STEM Road Map Curriculum Series* are designed in a similar manner, and NSTA Press and Routledge have published additional volumes in this series for this and other grade levels, and have plans to publish more.

For an up-to-date list of volumes in the series, please visit www.routledge.com/ STEM-Road-Map-Curriculum-Series/book-series/SRM (for titles co-published by Routledge and NSTA Press), or https://www.nsta.org/book-series/stem-road-map-curriculum (for titles published by NSTA Press).

If you are interested in professional development opportunities focused on the STEM Road Map specifically or integrated STEM or STEM programs and schools overall, contact the lead editor of this project, Dr. Carla C. Johnson, Professor of Science Education at NC State University (carlacjohnson@ncsu.edu). Someone from the team will be in touch to design a program that will meet your individual, school, or district needs.

APPENDIX A

STEM RESEARCH NOTEBOOK

MY STEM RESEARCH NOTEBOOK

OUR CHANGING ENVIRONMENT

NAME:

_____

_____

STEM Research Notebook #1 (Lesson Plan 1)

NAME _____

Draw and label two different habitats you saw in the video we watched

STEM Research Notebook #2 (Lesson Plan 1)

NAME _____

VOCABULARY WORDS

Word	Definition	Illustration

STEM Research Notebook #3 (Lesson Plan 1)

NAME _____

I learned . . .

_____

- -

_____

_____

- -

_____

_____

- -

_____

STEM Research Notebook #4 (Lesson Plan 1)

NAME _____

I learned . . .

_____
- -
_____

_____
- -
_____

_____
- -
_____

STEM Research Notebook #5, (Lesson Plan 1)

Bottle Labels

Use tape to attach one of the following labels to each of the 3 bottles:

STEM Research Notebook #5, page 2, (Lesson Plan 1)

NAME _____

Super Sunflowers - PREDICT

Circle your predictions.

Investigation #1: *This seed will get water and sun*

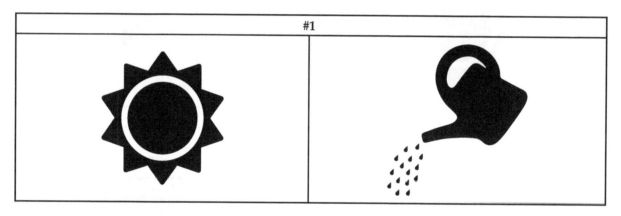

QUESTIONS	PREDICTIONS
What does your seed need to sprout into a seedling?	Light Water Both
How long will it take for your seed to sprout into a seedling?	About one day About one week About one month
How much will your seedling grow each week?	About one inch About one foot About one yard

STEM Research Notebook #5, page 3 (Lesson Plan 1)

NAME _____

Super Sunflowers – PREDICT

Investigation #2: **_This seed will get water but no sun_**

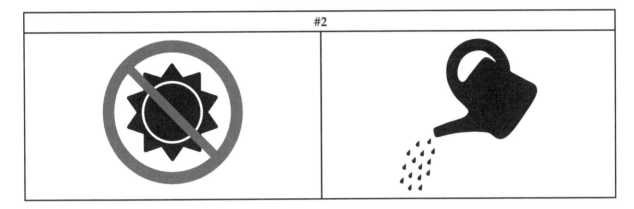

QUESTIONS	PREDICTIONS
What does your seed need to sprout into a seedling?	Light Water Both
How long will it take for your seed to sprout into a seedling?	About one day About one week About one month
How much will your seedling grow each week?	About one inch About one foot About one yard

APPENDIX A

STEM Research Notebook #5, page 4 (Lesson Plan 1)

NAME _____

Super Sunflowers – PREDICT

Investigation #3: _This seed will not be watered but will get sun_

QUESTIONS	PREDICTIONS
What does your seed need to sprout into a seedling?	Light Water Both
How long will it take for your seed to sprout into a seedling?	About one day About one week About one month
How much will your seedling grow each week?	About one inch About one foot About one yard

STEM Research Notebook #6 (Lesson Plan 1 - Ongoing)

NAME _____

Super Sunflowers – OBSERVATION 1

Measure the height of your plants and draw pictures

Investigation #1 (This seed got water and sun)

HEIGHT MEASURED:_____

Picture:

Investigation #2 (This seed got water but no sun)

HEIGHT MEASURED:_____

Picture:

Investigation #3 (This seed got no water but got sun)

HEIGHT MEASURED:_____

Picture:

APPENDIX A

STEM Research Notebook #6, page 2 (Lesson Plan 1 - Ongoing)

NAME_____

Super Sunflowers – OBSERVATION 2

Measure the height of your plants and draw pictures

Investigation #1 (This seed got water and sun)

HEIGHT MEASURED:_____

Picture:

Investigation #2 (This seed got water but no sun)

HEIGHT MEASURED:_____

Picture:

Investigation #3 (This seed got no water but got sun)

HEIGHT MEASURED:_____

Picture:

NATIONAL SCIENCE TEACHING ASSOCIATION

STEM Research Notebook #6, page 3 (Lesson Plan 1 - Ongoing)

Super Sunflowers – OBSERVATION 3

Measure the height of your plants and draw pictures

Investigation #1 (This seed got water and sun)

HEIGHT MEASURED:_____

Picture:

Investigation #2 (This seed got water but no sun)

HEIGHT MEASURED:_____

Picture:

Investigation #3 (This seed got no water but got sun)

HEIGHT MEASURED:_____

Picture:

STEM Research Notebook #6, page 4 (Lesson Plan 1 - Ongoing)

NAME_____

_____

Super Sunflowers – OBSERVATION 4

Measure the height of your plants and draw pictures

Investigation #1 (This seed got water and sun)

HEIGHT MEASURED:_____

Picture:

Investigation #2 (This seed got water but no sun)

HEIGHT MEASURED:_____

Picture:

Investigation #3 (This seed got no water but got sun)

HEIGHT MEASURED:_____

Picture:

STEM Research Notebook #7 (Lesson Plan 1)

NAME_____

Super Sunflowers - EXPLAIN

QUESTIONS	ANSWER	WHAT DID YOU OBSERVE?
What did your seeds need to sprout into a seedlings?		
How long did it take for your seeds to sprout into a seedlings?		
How much did your seedlings grow from the time you planted them until now?		

STEM Research Notebook #8 (Lesson Plan 2)

NAME_____

I learned . . .

_____

_ _

_____

_____

_ _

_____

_____

_ _

_____

STEM Research Notebook #9 (Lesson Plan 2)

NAME_____

I learned . . .

STEM Research Notebook #10 (Lesson Plan 2)

NAME_____

Our Neighborhood Habitat

What state do we live in?

_____

- -

_____

What city or town do we live in?

_____

- -

_____

Color in the state where we live:

STEM Research Notebook #10, page 2 (Lesson Plan 2)

NAME_____

What is the habitat like in our community?

Circle the kind of community where your school is:
City

Town

Rural (open space and farms)

Circle the things in nature that are near your community:
Forest

Desert

Prairie or grassland

Mountain

Ocean

Lake

River

STEM Research Notebook #10, page 3 (Lesson Plan 2)

NAME_____

Draw a picture of the neighborhood where your school is located.

NATIONAL SCIENCE TEACHING ASSOCIATION

STEM Research Notebook #10, page 4 (Lesson Plan 2)

NAME_____

What is the climate like where we live?

Circle the answer to these questions:

How often does it usually snow in the winter?

Never

1, 2, or 3 times all winter

4, 5, or 6 times all winter

There is usually snow on the ground all winter

Do you wear shorts and short sleeved shirts in the winter?

Yes   No

Do you wear shorts and short sleeved shirts in the summer?

Yes   No

Do the leaves change colors and fall off the trees in the fall?

Yes   No

STEM Research Notebook #10, page 5 (Lesson Plan 2)

NAME_____

What is the weather like now?

Draw a picture that shows the weather today where we live.

```



```

What season of the year is it?

_____

_____

What can you see or feel outside that helps you know what the season is?

_____

_____

STEM Research Notebook #11 (Lesson Plan 2)

NAME_____

Our Neighborhood Habitat

Count how many animals and insects you see.

How many did you count?_____

Draw and label two animals or insects you saw.

STEM Research Notebook #11, page 2 (Lesson Plan 2)

NAME_____

Our Neighborhood Habitat

Count how many plants you see.

How many did you count?_____

Draw and label two plants you saw.

STEM Research Notebook #11, page 3 (Lesson Plan 2)

NAME_____

Our Neighborhood Habitat

Draw and label things that made two sounds you heard.

STEM Research Notebook #11, page 4 (Lesson Plan 2)

NAME_____

Our Neighborhood Habitat

Draw and label two things that you smelled.

STEM Research Notebook #11, page 5 (Lesson Plan 2)

NAME_____

Our Neighborhood Habitat

Draw and label two ways that weather affects animals, plants, and the people where we live.

STEM Research Notebook #11, page 6 (Lesson Plan 2)

NAME_____

Our Neighborhood Habitat

Draw and label two ways that people have harmed the environment in the school neighborhood.

STEM Research Notebook #11, page 7 (Lesson Plan 2)

NAME_____

Our Neighborhood Habitat

Draw and label two ways that people have improved the environment in the school neighborhood.

STEM Research Notebook #12 (Lesson Plan 2)

NAME_____

I learned . . .

_____

- -

_____

_____

- -

_____

_____

- -

_____

NATIONAL SCIENCE TEACHING ASSOCIATION

STEM Research Notebook #13 (Lesson Plan 3)

NAME_____

I learned . . .

_____

_____

_____

_____

_____

_____

STEM Research Notebook #14 (Lesson Plan 3)

NAME_____

I learned . . .

_____

_____
_____

_____
_____

_____

STEM Research Notebook #15 (Lesson Plan 3)

NAME_____

I learned . . .

_____

_____

_____

_____

_____

_____

My Environment News Template

NATIONAL SCIENCE TEACHING ASSOCIATION

My Environment News

Name:

_____

_____

HABITATS

Name the state where your school is located

_____
- -
_____

Name the city or town where your school is located

_____
- -
_____

Color in the state where you live

Copyright material from Carla C. Johnson, Janet B. Walton, and Erin E. Peters-Burton (2022) *Our Changing Environment, Grade K: STEM Road Map for Elementary School*, Routledge

Weather

Draw a picture of the weather today.

Climate

Draw a picture of what the trees around your school look like in the winter

Draw a picture of the kind of clothes you wear in the winter where you live

Animals and Insects

Draw and label two animals or insects that live in the habitat near your school

1.

_____

_____

Animals and Insects

2.

_____

_____

Plants

Draw and label three types of plants that live in your local habitat:

1.

_____

_____

Plants

2.

_____

_____

Plants

3.

_____

- -

_____

Good Neighbors

Our class cared for our neighborhood environment. Draw what your class did to care for the school neighborhood environment:

Use words to describe what our class did to care for the neighborhood environment.

_____

_____

_____

_____

What are three things other people can do to care for the school environment?

1.

_____

- -

_____

_____

- -

_____

2.

_____

- -

_____

_____

- -

_____

3.

_____

- -

_____

_____

- -

_____

Draw and label one thing people can do to improve the environment in the school neighborhood

_____

_____

Draw and label one thing people can do to improve the environment in the school neighborhood

_____

_____

Draw and label one thing people can do to improve the environment in the school neighborhood

_____

_____

NATIONAL SCIENCE TEACHING ASSOCIATION

APPENDIX B

Table B. Rubrics: OBSERVATION, STEM RESEARCH NOTEBOOK, AND PARTICIPATION

OBSERVATION, STEM RESEARCH NOTEBOOK, AND PARTICIPATION RUBRIC						
Name:_____			Date:_____			
Categories (components)	0 Missing or unrelated	1 Beginning	2 Developing	3 Meets expectations	4 Exceeds expectation	TOTAL
Observation of listening and discussion skills	Component is missing or unrelated.	Does not listen to others and shows little respect for alternative viewpoints.	Occasionally listens to others but often speaks out of turn.	Listens to others, only occasionally speaks out of turn, and generally accepts other points of view.	Listens carefully to others, waits for turn to speak, and respects alternative viewpoints.	
STEM Research Notebook	Component is missing or unrelated.	Indicates little understanding of the concepts being taught.	Recalls and is able to explain basic facts and concepts.	Demonstrates ability to apply concepts, using information in new situations.	Demonstrates a deep understanding of concepts by drawing relationships between ideas and using information to generate new ideas.	
Participation	Component is missing.	Does not volunteer. When responding to teacher prompts, comments are sometimes not relevant to the discussion.	Responds to teacher prompts during classroom discussions but does not volunteer.	Willingly participates in classroom discussions and offers relevant comments.	Contributes insightful comments and poses thoughtful questions.	
TOTAL						

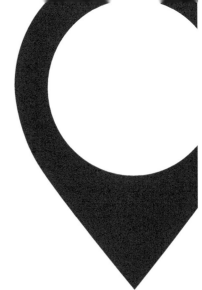

APPENDIX C

CONTENT STANDARDS ADDRESSED
IN THIS MODULE

NEXT GENERATION SCIENCE STANDARDS

Table C1 (p. 154) lists the science and engineering practices, disciplinary core ideas, and crosscutting concepts this module addresses. The supported performance expectations are as follows:

- K-LS1–1. Use observations to describe patterns of what plants and animals (including humans) need to survive.

- K-ESS2–1. Use and share observations of local weather conditions to describe patterns over time.

- K-ESS2–2. Construct an argument supported by evidence for how plants and animals (including humans) can change the environment to meet their needs.

- K-ESS3–1. Use a model to represent the relationship between the needs of different plants and animals (including humans) and the places they live.

- K-PS3–1. Make observations to determine the effect of sunlight on Earth's surface.

Table C1. Next Generation Science Standards (NGSS)

Science and Engineering Practices

ANALYZING AND INTERPRETING DATA
- Analyzing data in K–2 builds on prior experiences and progresses to collecting, recording, and sharing observations.
- Use observations (firsthand or from media) to describe patterns in the natural world in order to answer scientific questions.

DEVELOPING AND USING MODELS
- Modeling in K–2 builds on prior experiences and progresses to include using and developing models (i.e., diagram, drawing, physical replica, diorama, dramatization, storyboard) that represent concrete events or design solutions.
- Use a model to represent relationships in the natural world.

PLANNING AND CARRYING OUT INVESTIGATIONS
- Planning and carrying out investigations to answer questions or test solutions to problems in K–2 builds on prior experiences and progresses to simple investigations, based on fair tests, which provide data to support explanations or design solutions.
- Make observations (firsthand or from media) to collect data that can be used to make comparisons.

Disciplinary Core Ideas

LS1.C. ORGANIZATION FOR MATTER AND ENERGY FLOW IN ORGANISMS
- All animals need food in order to live and grow. They obtain their food from plants or from other animals. Plants need water and light to live and grow.

ESS3.A. NATURAL RESOURCES
- Living things need water, air, and resources from the land, and they live in places that have the things they need. Humans use natural resources for everything they do.

PS3.B. CONSERVATION OF ENERGY AND ENERGY TRANSFER
- Sunlight warms Earth's surface.

Crosscutting Concepts

PATTERNS
- Patterns in the natural and human designed world can be observed and used as evidence.

SYSTEMS AND SYSTEM MODELS
- Systems in the natural and designed world have parts that work together.

CAUSE AND EFFECT
- Events have causes that generate observable patterns.

Table C2. Common Core Mathematics and English Language Arts (ELA) Standards

Common Core State Standards for Mathematics	Common Core State Standards for English Language Arts
MATHEMATICAL PRACTICES MP1. Make sense of problems and persevere in solving them. MP2. Reason abstractly and quantitatively. MP3. Construct viable arguments and critique the reasoning of others. MP4. Model with mathematics. MP5. Use appropriate tools strategically. MP6. Attend to precision. MP7. Look for and make use of structure. MP8. Look for and express regularity in repeated reasoning. MATHEMATICAL CONTENT K.CC.B.4. Understand the relationship between numbers and quantities; connect counting to cardinality. K.CC.B.4a. When counting objects, say the number names in the standard order, pairing each object with one and only one number name and each number name with one and only one object. K.CC.B.4b. Understand that the last number name said tells the number of objects counted. The number of objects is the same regardless of their arrangement or the order in which they were counted. K.CC.B.4c. Understand that each successive number name refers to a quantity that is one larger. K.CC.C.6. Identify whether the number of objects in one group is greater than, less than, or equal to the number of objects in another group, e.g., by using matching and counting strategies. K.CC.C.7. Compare two numbers between 1 and 10 presented as written numerals. K.MD.A.1. Describe measurable attributes of objects, such as length or weight. Describe several measurable attributes of a single object. K.MD.A.2. Directly compare two objects with a measurable attribute in common, to see which object has "more of"/"less of" the attribute, and describe the difference. For example, directly compare the heights of two children and describe one child as taller/shorter. K.MD.B.3. Classify objects into given categories; count the numbers of objects in each category and sort the categories by count.	READING STANDARDS RI.K.1. With prompting and support, ask and answer questions about key details in a text. RI.K.3. With prompting and support, describe the connection between two individuals, events, ideas, or pieces of information in a text. WRITING STANDARDS W.K.2 Use a combination of drawing, dictating, and writing to compose informative/explanatory texts in which they name what they are writing about and supply some information about the topic. W.K.5 With guidance and support from adults, respond to questions and suggestions from peers and add details to strengthen writing as needed. W.K.7 Participate in shared research and writing projects (e.g., explore a number of books by a favorite author and express opinions about them). SPEAKING AND LISTENING STANDARDS SL.K.1. Participate in collaborative conversations with diverse partners about kindergarten topics and texts with peers and adults in small and larger groups. SL.K.3. Ask and answer questions in order to seek help, get information, or clarify something that is not understood. SL.K.5. Add drawings or other visual displays to descriptions as desired to provide additional detail.

Table C3. National Association for the Education of Young Children (NAEYC) Standards

NAEYC Curriculum Content Area for Cognitive Development: Science and Technology
2.G.02. Children are provided varied opportunities and materials to learn key content and principles of science.
2.G.03. Children are provided with varied opportunities and materials that encourage them to use the five senses to observe, explore, and experiment with scientific phenomena.
2.G.04. Children are provided with varied opportunities to use simple tools to observe objects and scientific phenomena.
2.G.05. Children are provided with varied opportunities and materials to collect data and to represent and document their findings (e.g., through drawing or graphing).
2.G.06. Children are provided with varied opportunities and materials that encourage them to think, question, and reason about observed and inferred phenomena.
2.G.07. Children are provided with varied opportunities and materials that encourage them to discuss scientific concepts in everyday conversation.
2.G.08. Children are provided with varied opportunities and materials that help them learn and use scientific terminology and vocabulary associated with the content areas.
2.H.02. All children have opportunities to access technology that they can use.
2.H.03. Technology is used to extend learning within the classroom and integrate and enrich the curriculum.

Table C4. 21st Century Skills From the Framework for 21st Century Learning

21st Century Skills	Learning Skills and Technology Tools	Teaching Strategies	Evidence of Success
Interdisciplinary themes	Health Literacy Environmental Literacy	• Provide students with the opportunity to investigate the local environment with a focus on human impacts on the environment and their effects on plant and animal habitats. • Provide students with the opportunity to explore various types of pollution and their effects on the environment.	• Students communicate their observations about the local environment and human impacts on the environment. • Students complete a project to impact the local environment in positive ways.
Learning and innovation skills	Creativity and Innovation Critical Thinking and Problem Solving Communication and Collaboration	• Facilitate creativity and innovation through having students design and create toys from waste materials. • Facilitate creativity and innovation through having students design and create a newsletter or blog. • Provide students with opportunities to practice communication skills through presenting the toys they created and through the content they create in their newsletter or blog. • Facilitate critical thinking and problem solving through use of the EDP and having students make observations in a real-world setting about their local environment.	• Students demonstrate creativity and innovation, critical thinking, and problem solving as they design and create their toys and as they design and create their newsletter or blog. • Students work collaboratively and communicate effectively in teams to complete a group project.

Continued

Table C4. *(continued)*

21st Century Skills	Learning Skills and Technology Tools	Teaching Strategies	Evidence of Success
Information, media, and technology skills	Information Literacy Media Literacy Information Communication and Technology Literacy	• Engage students in guided practice and scaffolding strategies through the use of developmentally appropriate books, videos, and websites to advance their knowledge. • Scaffold student work to create content in a newsletter or blog to communicate information to a targeted audience.	• Students acquire and use deeper content knowledge as they work to complete their newsletter or blog. • Students communicate their content knowledge effectively to the target audience.
Life and career skills	Flexibility and Adaptability Initiative and Self-Direction Social and Cross Cultural Skills Productivity and Accountability Leadership and Responsibility	• Facilitate student collaborative teamwork to foster life and career skills.	• Throughout the module, students collaborate as they work on group projects.

NATIONAL SCIENCE TEACHING ASSOCIATION

Table C5. English Language Development Standards

English Language Development Standards: Grades pre-K-5 (WIDA, 2012)

ELD Standard 1: Social and Instructional Language
    English language learners communicate for Social and Instructional purposes within the school setting.
ELD Standard 2: The Language of Language Arts
    English language learners communicate information, ideas and concepts necessary for academic success in the content area of Language Arts.
ELD Standard 3: The Language of Mathematics
    English language learners communicate information, ideas and concepts necessary for academic success in the content area of Mathematics
ELD Standard 4: The Language of Science.
    English language learners communicate information, ideas and concepts necessary for academic success in the content area of Science
ELD Standard 5: The Language of Social Studies
    English language learners communicate information, ideas and concepts necessary for academic success in the content area of Social Studies.

Source: WIDA, 2012. 2012 Amplification of the English language development standards: Kindergarten–grade 12, *https://wida.wisc.edu.*

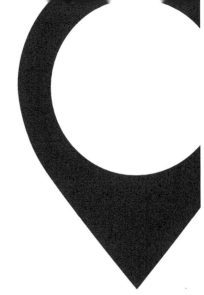

INDEX

Page nos. in *Italics* represent Figures
Page nos. in **Bold** represent Tables

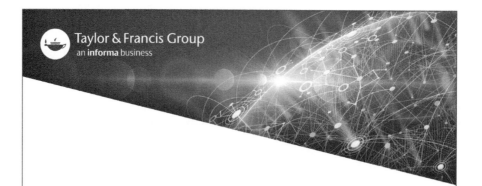

For Product Safety Concerns and Information please contact our
EU representative GPSR@taylorandfrancis.com Taylor & Francis
Verlag GmbH, Kaufingerstraße 24, 80331 München, Germany